GUINNESS

GUINNESS

ROBERT TANITCH

APPLAUSE
THEATRE BOOK PUBLISHERS

FOR PETER AND ROSEMARY HIRST

Also by Robert Tanitch

A Pictorial Companion to Shakespeare's Plays
Ralph Richardson, A Tribute
Olivier
Leonard Rossiter
Ashcroft
Gielgud
Dirk Bogarde

Copyright © Robert Tanitch 1989

Library of Congress Cataloging-in-Publication Data

Tanitch, Robert.
  Guinness

  Bibliography: p.
  Includes index.
  1. Guinness, Alec, 1914–   . 2. Guinness, Alec,
1914–   —Pictorial works. 3. Actors—Great Britain—
Biography. 4 Actors—Great Britain—Pictorial works.
I. Title
PN2598.G8T36 1989   792′.028′0924 [B] 89–274
ISBN 1–55783–042–8

APPLAUSE THEATRE BOOK PUBLISHERS
211 W. 71st St
New York, NY 10023
212/595–4735

Published by arrangement with Harrap Books Ltd.

First Applause printing, 1989

Printed in Great Britain

Frontispiece: *Alec Guinness in* The Bridge on the River Kwai *1957*

CONTENTS

CONTENTS

INTRODUCTION

Alec Guinness is acknowledged by the acting profession, public and critics alike to be one of the great actors of the twentieth century. This book, which celebrates his seventy-fifth birthday, is a pictorial record and full chronology of his career in theatre, film and television from the 1930s to the present day.

Guinness has said that he cannot remember a time when he did not want to act. He has appeared in plays by Shakespeare, Obey, Chekhov, Sheridan, Shaw, Pinero, Auden and Isherwood, Sartre, Rostand, Jonson, Feydeau, Ionesco, Durrenmatt and Miller.

He has created roles for Clemence Dane, J.B.Priestley, T.S.Eliot, Bridget Boland, Terence Rattigan, Daphne du Maurier, Simon Gray, John Mortimer and Alan Bennett.

In his time he has played a psychiatrist, painter, gardening reporter, tobacconist, bigamist, cardinal, pope, Bolshevik, suffragette, ghost, inventor, mayor, traitor, anaesthetist, POW, transvestite and mole-catcher.

He has also been a commercial traveller, photographic reconnaissance officer, philosophic hangman, blind barrister, blind butler, High Court judge, bogus major, illiterate half-caste, galactic knight, lecherous GP, Japanese millionaire, Spanish priest, Brahmin mystic and German air-raid warden.

He has robbed the Bank of England, quelled a mutiny, climbed a demon-haunted mountain (the demon turned out to be his mother), survived the *Titanic*, gone mad in Scotland, lost his head in London, discovered the elixir of life, and supplied MI6 with drawings of vacuum cleaners . . .

Alec Guinness was born in London on the 2 April 1914. He was educated at Pembroke Lodge School, Southbourne, and Roborough School, near Eastbourne. He left at eighteen to work for eighteen months as a junior copywriter in Ark's Publicity, an advertising agency in Lincoln's Inn Fields.

He trained for the theatre, initially having private lessons with the actress Martita Hunt, later famous for her Miss Havisham in *Great Expectations*. After five lessons she very nearly gave up, convinced they were both wasting their time. Some sixteen lessons later he won a two-year scholarship to the Fay Compton Studio of Dramatic Art where he was awarded first prize in their Annual Show by the adjudicators, John Gielgud, Jessie Matthews and Ronald Adam.

In 1934 while still a student he made his stage debut in Edward Wooll's court-room drama, *Libel!*, playing a Junior Counsel, a walk-on part. A few months later, having left the drama studio, unable to complete the course for lack of funds, he landed three cameo parts – Chinese coolie, French pirate and British sailor – in Noel Langley's *Queer Cargo*.

Opposite: The Man in the White Suit· *1951*

The Alchemist *1947*

John Gielgud invited him to join his company at the New Theatre. His roles included the Third Player and Osric in Gielgud's *Hamlet*, the wolf in André Obey's biblical pantomime for adults, *Noah*, Sampson and the Apothecary in the famous Gielgud-Olivier-Ashcroft *Romeo and Juliet*, and the workman and later Yakov in Anton Chekhov's *The Seagull*, directed by Theodore Komisarjevsky.

He then joined Tyrone Guthrie at the Old Vic for the 1936/37 season. He was cast as Boyet in *Love's Labour's Lost*, Le Beau and rustic William in *As You Like It*, Old Thorney in Thomas Dekker's *The Witch of Edmonton*, Reynaldo and Osric in Olivier's *Hamlet*, Sir Andrew Aguecheek in *Twelfth Night*, and the Duke of Exeter in *Henry V*. He disliked playing Boyet, loathed playing Le Beau, loved playing William, and scored a big success as Sir Andrew.

He returned to John Gielgud for his 1937/1938 season of four classics at the Queen's Theatre. His roles included Aumerle and the Groom in *Richard II*, Snake in Sheridan's *The School for Scandal*, Fedotik in Chekhov's *Three Sisters*, directed by Michel Saint-Denis, and Lorenzo in *The Merchant of Venice*. His speaking of Shakespeare's verse won high praise.

He was seen briefly in Bernard Shaw's *The Doctor's Dilemma* at the Richmond Theatre in Surrey, playing Louis Dubedat, before re-joining the Old Vic Company to play an impetuous and youthful Hamlet (he was twenty-four-years-old), an immensely likeable Bob Acres in Sheridan's *The Rivals*, and Arthur Gower, the unrewarding juvenile lead, in Arthur Wing Pinero's *Trelawny of the 'Wells'*. His Hamlet, acted in the Gielgud manner, produced in modern dress and in its entirety (in its eternity said the wags in the company), was touchingly naturalistic, deeply felt and beautifully spoken; but the general feeling was that he didn't yet have the power to sustain the role over four hours.

On his return from the Old Vic Company's tour of Egypt and Europe (in which he also played the Chorus in *Henry V* and Emile Flordon in *Libel!*) he acted in W.H.Auden and Christopher Isherwood's political and psychological verse drama, *The Ascent of F.6*, cast as the priggish hero. This he followed with *Romeo and Juliet* in Perth, his own adaptation of *Great Expectations*, Clemence Dane's flop *Cousin Muriel*, *The Tempest*, and a tour of Robert Ardrey's *Thunder Rock*, playing the lighthouse-keeper, a role created by Michael Redgrave.

With the advent of the Second World War he joined the Royal Navy and was commissioned in 1942. He was given leave of absence to make his American debut in *Flare Path*, Terence Rattigan's wartime propaganda piece and precursor to the much better and more famous film, *The Way to the Stars*. When the play flopped (New York theatregoers at that stage not being interested in Europe's war) he returned to active service, in time for the invasion of Sicily, when his craft was the first to land.

After the war he returned to the stage in his own adaptation of Dostoevsky's *The Brothers Karamazov*, playing a dissolute and reckless Mitya, which he followed with a neurotic and cowardly Garcin in Jean-Paul Sartre's *Vicious Circle* (better known as *Huis Clos*), both vividly directed by the then *enfant terrible*, the twenty-one-year-old Peter Brook.

In 1946 Guinness joined the legendary Laurence Olivier-Ralph Richardson Old Vic season at the New Theatre. (The Old Vic Theatre had been bombed during the war.) His roles included the Fool in *King Lear*, Eric Brilling in J.B. Priestley's morality play, *An Inspector Calls*, de Guiche, an elegant and stylish villain, in Edmond Rostand's *Cyrano de Bergerac*, and Abel Drugger, the tobacconist suffering from halitosis, in Ben Jonson's *The Alchemist*. The Fool, a chalk-white-faced clown with one eyebrow, was one of his favourite parts. 'Even I couldn't pretend I wasn't successful,' he would tell Robert Cushman years later in an interview for the *Radio Times*. 'But that's mainly because I only played half the part. Larry was directing and he said, "A lot of it's very boring, old dear," and cut it.' The role was trimmed to twelve lines of actual speech.

He stayed on for a second season to play a Gielgudish Richard II, in an unhelpful production by Ralph Richardson, an impudent and penniless Hlestikov in Nikolai Gogol's classic case of mistaken identity, *The Government Inspector*, an endearingly comic Dauphin opposite Celia Johnson's light-weight Maid in Bernard Shaw's *Saint Joan*, and finally a white-haired, wise and humorous Menenius in *Coriolanus*, stealing most of the notices.

These eight roles, in their breadth, made an enormous impression on critics and public alike. He was likened to the great actor Joseph Shepherd Munden (1758–1832) of whose face Charles Lamb wrote: 'Munden has none that you can properly pin down and call *his*. . . He is not one, but legion. Not so much a comedian, as a company. If his name could be multiplied like his countenance, it might fill a playbill.'

His West End engagement in J.Lee-Thompson and Dudley Leslie's *The Human Touch*, the story of Dr James Simpson, the first surgeon to use chloroform as an anaesthetic, was followed by the much more rewarding *The Cocktail Party*, T.S. Eliot's Christian ritual of redemption, first seen at the Edinburgh Festival in 1949 and later, with great success, in New York, though sadly not in London (at least not with Guinness) for another eighteen years. He described his role of metaphysical psychiatrist as demanding more concentration than anything he had ever attempted.

Back in the West End in 1951, his unromantic, low-keyed, bearded Hamlet was certainly not helped by the lighting board having a disastrous attack of first night nerves. Day scenes were played in pitch darkness and night scenes were played in broad daylight. Beverley Baxter, writing in the *Evening Standard*, said it was the worst *Hamlet* he had ever seen.

He had as many roles as an insect has feet in Sam and Bella Spewack's insect fable, *Under the Sycamore Tree*. His invention and mocking wit in what amounted to a series of revue turns were enjoyed more than the play, which was pretty thin stuff.

In 1953 he joined Tyrone Guthrie in Canada to inaugurate Stratford Ontario's first Festival of Shakespeare in their brand new theatre with *Richard III*, and the King of France in a modern dress production of *All's Well That Ends Well*.

He scored a notable success as the hard, proud, unlovable cardinal, in Bridget Boland's *The Prisoner*, a man of intellect rather than feeling, playing on the minds rather than the emotions of the audience.

Two years later in 1956 he was seen in the French farce *Hotel Paradiso* by Georges Feydeau and Maurice Desvallières. The play, directed and acted with clockwork precision, was great fun, and would lead to a seemingly unending supply of Feydeau farces over the next thirty years.

His performance as T.E. Lawrence (a role he had long wanted to play) in Terence Rattigan's *Ross* matched the author's characteristic understatement, and won him the *Evening Standard*'s drama award for best actor in 1960. His performance as the dying king in Eugene Ionesco's *Exit the King* won him the *Plays and Players* award in 1963.

He then went to America to play Dylan Thomas in Sidney Michaels's *Dylan*, where his performance (described by *Newsweek* as 'a triumph of Thespian skill over eccentric miscasting') won him a 'Tony' award in 1964.

On his return to England he played the homosexual Austrian prince, half in love with death, in *Incident at Vichy*, Arthur Miller's debate on the Final Solution.

The Prisoner *1954*

The Cocktail Party *1968*

In 1962 he was quoted as saying he would have liked to have done a modern dress Lear or Macbeth 'but only where nobody could hear or see me'. In 1968 he was seen very publicly at the Royal Court Theatre in a Brechtian production of *Macbeth* which managed to alienate practically everybody.

The following year he appeared as a transvestite criminal-on-the-run in Simon Gray's *Wise Child*, a black comedy in the kinky Joe Orton manner which, despite the funny lines and the gratis West Indian strip-tease, was a bit of a drag.

He returned to *The Cocktail Party* in 1968 at the Chichester Festival Theatre. His production, crystal clear and beautifully spoken, transferred successfully to the West End. Once again it was his spiritual authority which was so impressive.

He had a long and exhausting role as a chemist who had discovered the elixir of life in Bridget Boland's *Time Out of Mind* which was seen at the Yvonne Arnaud Theatre in Guildford in 1970. He then played John Mortimer's blind barrister father in *A Voyage Round My Father* (1971). His performance, remarkable for its convincing physical detail, was perhaps more benign than might have been expected, given the caustic malice of the text.

He scored a big success in two plays by Alan Bennett. In the first, *Habeas Corpus* (1973), a stylised and witty piece, he played a philandering doctor who fancies his patients. In the second, *The Old Country* (1977), a characteristic Bennettian mixture of nostalgia, parody and irony, he was cast as a burnt-out traitor-in-exile, who does an excellent demolishing job on E.M. Forster's famous aphorism about betraying either one's country or one's friend.

In between he was seen in a stylish but lifeless adaptation of Ivy Compton-Burnett's *A Family and A Fortune* (1975), and in an entertaining anthology of Jonathan Swift's writings, *Yahoo* (1976).

His most recent roles have been Shylock in *The Merchant of Venice* (1984) at Chichester Festival Theatre, and the Russian diplomat in Brian Blessing's two-hander, *A Walk in the Woods* (1988), a conversation piece on nuclear disarmament, acted with characteristic economy.

Guinness's career in the cinema began in 1934 while he was still at drama school when he worked for one day as an extra on the Evelyn Laye musical, *Evensong*. It was not an experience he enjoyed.

His real debut came in 1946 with Herbert Pocket in *Great Expectations*, which he followed two years later with an unforgettable Fagin in *Oliver Twist*. Both films were directed by David Lean, and their working relationship would continue through into the 1980s.

Kind Hearts and Coronets (1949) was such a *tour de force* – he played eight roles – that the film, a brilliant black comedy, came (very unfairly to Dennis Price) to be thought of as his film.

He was seen in *A Run for Your Money* (1949), *Last Holiday* (1950) and *The Mudlark* (1950). His authority and finesse as Benjamin Disraeli in the latter was particularly admired. It was a role he had played many years previously in an impersonation of George Arliss when he was auditioning to get into drama school.

His next two films, the immensely popular Ealing Comedies, *The Lavender Hill Mob* (1951) and *the Man in the White Suit* (1951), set their seal on Guinness's fame at home and abroad, and would lead *Time Magazine* to

The Lavender Hill Mob *1951*

Tunes of Glory *1960*

describe him as 'one of our most subtle and profound clowns since Chaplin'.

He was then seen as Denry Manchin in a likeable adaptation of Arnold Bennett's *The Card* (1952). He played the romantic lead in *Malta Story* (1953) and the bigamist in *The Captain's Paradise* (1953). He was more convincing as the dull husband than the cha-cha-ing lover with a flower in his teeth.

He followed these two Mediterranean capers with an up-dated version of *Father Brown* (1954), *To Paris with Love* (1955), an ineffectual farce, and *The Prisoner* (1955), a record of his stage performance, which made the mistake of trying to open the play out.

The juxtaposition of burly, inarticulate, murderous thieves and bird-like, twittering old ladies in *The Ladykillers* (1955), another classic Ealing Comedy, provided a hilarious setting for his memorable disguise as the loony Professor Marcus who is finally, with neat poetic justice, given the chop by a dropping railway signal.

He made his Hollywood debut in 1956 in the glossy elegance of Ferenc Molnar's Ruritanian comedy *The Swan*, acting opposite Grace Kelly in her last film before she married Prince Rainier of Monaco.

His next film, *The Bridge on the River Kwai* (1957), a dramatisation of the building of the notorious Burma-Siam 'Death Railway' in the Second World War, made him an international star. His performance as Colonel Nicholson, so blinkered in his obsession, patriotism and racial arrogance that he actually collaborates with the Japanese, won him many awards, including an 'Oscar'.

He followed this epic statement on the folly of war with a return to small-scale Ealing Comedy in *Barnacle Bill*, a film which sank with all hands in a sea of whimsy.

His next role was the painter-genius Gulley Jimson in his own adaptation and script of Joyce Cary's *The Horse's Mouth* (1958). Though he won the Venice Film Festival Award for the best actor and an 'Oscar' nomination for his script, the film was badly underrated on both sides of the Atlantic. *The Times Educational Supplement*, for instance, accused him of turning Gulley's 'pantheistic exhuberance into mere eccentricity', while *Time Magazine* felt he 'simply lacked the demonic force to fill out a personality as large as Jimson's'. The film's rehabilitation is long overdue.

Nobody, including Guinness himself, was happy with *The Scapegoat* (1959), which he co-produced with the author Daphne du Maurier, and in which he played a French count and his English double. He fared little better in Graham Greene's political thriller, *Our Man in Havana* (1959), where he was accused of being colourless when the whole point about the diffident vacuum cleaner salesman he was playing was that he was meant to be colourless. The characters round him, all larger than life, provided the colour.

He then went on to score one of his major screen successes as the bluff, breezy, cany Scots soldier in James Kennaway's *Tunes of Glory* (1960), an extrovert role quite unlike anything he had played before and which had been earmarked for his co-star John Mills until the two agreed to swap parts.

He looked ill at ease as a Japanese millionaire in the synthetic schmaltz of *A Majority of One* (1961), and not much happier as the kind-hearted captain of a frigate in *HMS Defiant* (1962), a schoolboy adventure set during the Spithead mutinies of 1797.

He appeared in three block-busting epics: as Prince Feisal in *Lawrence of Arabia* (1962), as Marcus Aurelius in *The Fall of the Roman Empire* (1964 –

which gave the unfortunate impression that if only Sophia Loren and Stephen Boyd had not run off together the Roman Empire would have been saved), and as Yevgraf in *Doctor Zhivago* (1965). He also appeared in two block-emptying comedies: *Situation Hopeless – But Not Serious* (1965), and *Hotel Paradiso* (1966) which should never have left the stage.

He had a small but important role in *The Quiller Memorandum* (1966) which he played with crisp ruthlessness and chilling detachment. He was also seen as the braggart Jones, a bogus major, all phoney bonhommie and glib clichés, in *The Comedians* (1967).

Guinness had long wanted to play Charles I. He finally did so with cavalier restraint in *Cromwell* (1970), keeping his melancholy head while all around him were shouting themselves hoarse.

He appeared as a whey-faced Old Marley in the family musical *Scrooge* (1970) and as the Pope (replacing Laurence Olivier) in *Fratello Sole, Sorella Luna* (1972), Franco Zeffirelli's handsomely mounted religious kitsch on the subject of St Francis of Assisi.

There was a fearful row when Bernard Delfont banned *Hitler – The Last Ten Days* from all 265 cinemas on the ABC circuit in 1973. The film, fatally uncertain of its approach to an already uneasy mixture of melodrama and documentary, often ended up in farce.

He was very funny as the blind butler in the Neil Simon spoof detective story *Murder by Death* (1976), and the Force certainly was with him when he agreed to be in George Lucas's galactic top-grosser *Star Wars* (1977), his earnings (he was on a percentage) coming in for as much comment as his acting.

He played one of the survivors in the eminently sinkable *Raise the Titanic* (1980) and a fantasy Freud, with phallic cigar, in the Dudley Moore vehicle, *Lovesick* (1983). His appearance as a Brahmin mystic in *A Passage to India* (1984) was embarrassing, the general feeling being that the days when white actors browned-up had long since passed.

His two most recent roles have been Mr Dorrit, the 'Father of Marshalsea' in *Little Dorrit* (1987) – universally acclaimed as one of his finest screen performances – and the crazy, illiterate half-caste, Mr Todd, who provides *A Handful of Dust* (1988) with its disturbing and unforgettable climax.

Cromwell *1970*

Guinness made his first appearance on television in 1955 on the opening night of the commercial channel when he was seen in *Baker's Dozen*, a brief Edwardian sketch by 'Saki' (H.H. Munro) about a widow and widower who, though keen to marry, are put off by the fact that they have thirteen children between them.

He made his American debut in 1958 as a mild bank clerk causing chaos to the book-keeping system in John D. Hess's comedy *The Wicked Scheme of Jebal Deeks*. Ten years later in England he played a philosophical hangman in *Conversation at Night*, Friedrich Durrenmatt's turgid and Kafkaesque allegory of death.

The commercial channel had so little faith in *Twelfth Night* (in which he was Malvolio) that they delayed showing it for two years, and then only put it on late at night.

Apart from two *Solo* programmes in which he read the verse of e.e. cummings and *Little Gidding* by T.S. Eliot, he was not seen again until 1974 in John Osborne's *A Gift of Friendship*. He played a celebrated writer who

Tinker, Tailor, Soldier, Spy *1979*

invites a former colleague, a man he has long despised, to be his literary executor. James Thomas, in the *Daily Express*, was not impressed by the play: 'Not all Sir Alec's skill could bring this pretentious dialogue to life.'

In 1977 he appeared in a truncated version of Bernard Shaw's *Caesar and Cleopatra*, cast as emperor and father-figure to Genevieve Bujold's sex-kitten.

He was the flint-hearted Earl of Dorincourt in the third and unexpectedly witty and moving version of *Little Lord Fauntleroy* (1980). The famous velvet suit (originally based on a costume worn by Oscar Wilde when he visited the author during his American tour) came out of the closet only once. As for the famous curls, anathema even to those who had never read the novel, they had been cut.

He made something which was both sad and funny out of a prim High Court judge's vulnerability in John Mortimer's *Edwin* (1984).

It was Graham Greene who suggested he should play Father Quixote in *Monsignor Quixote* (1985), a modern Cervantian road movie. Guinness didn't see how he could possibly play a Spanish priest and wondered what he should look and sound like. In the end he played him absolutely straight – so straight that at times it seemed as if the camera was invading his privacy.

His most famous television role remains George Smiley, first seen in the circumlocutory and elusive *Tinker, Tailor, Soldier, Spy* (1979), John Le Carré's elegaic metaphor for Britain and institutional life, a sophisticated parlour game for members of the secret service. Three years later Smiley was back, a sadder, more single-minded, more aggressive figure, in *Smiley's People*, which proved equally compulsive viewing. So identified is he with the role that it is very difficult now to imagine anybody else in the part, even though, of course, he is nothing like the George Smiley in the novel.

Smiley was one of Guinness's most subtle performances. For some people the pared-down performance was evidently too subtle. ('Dullness is now his speciality,' wrote Russell Davies in the *Sunday Times*.) He had mastered the art of doing nothing so well that, not for the first time in his career, it seemed as if he wasn't acting at all.

Alec Guinness, the least obtrusive of actors, believing the less he does the better, cuts out the dramatic flourishes and relies on the tiniest physical and vocal inflections to make his effects. His low-keyed, economical performances, with their impeccable timing and subtle use of irony and understatement, have long been admired by the acting profession, critics and public alike.

The pages which follow are a pictorial record of his distinguished career and a tribute to his authority, versatility, precision and consummate technical skill. They are also a tribute to the man himself – an acknowledgement of the enormous pleasure his acting has given over six decades.

Opposite: *Alec Guinness in* Hamlet *1938*

1930s

LIBEL! – 1934

Aubrey Mather as the Judge, Frances Doble in the dock, Basil Dignam at the table below the Judge, Beckett Bould in tunic and Anthony Hollis next to him, and standing, Leon M. Lion and Nigel Playfair as the two counsels in Edward Wooll's Libel!, directed by Leon M. Lion at the Playhouse Theatre.

THIS PRODUCTION marked Guinness's first appearance on the stage. He was cast in the non-speaking role of a Junior Counsel, and he is sitting directly behind Nigel Playfair!

He appeared in *Libel!* again five years later when he was the Old Vic Company's leading man and touring Europe and Egypt in Shakespeare and Sheridan. The Egyptian authorities specifically asked for the play. It was evidently an examination set-text.

HAMLET – 1934

Top: George Howe as Polonius, Richard Dare, Ian Atkins, Alec Guinness, Sam Beazley and George Devine as the Players, John Gielgud as Hamlet, Richard Ainley as Rosencrantz and Anthony Quayle as Guildenstern in Shakespeare's Hamlet, directed by John Gielgud at the New Theatre.

Bottom: Frank Vosper as Claudius, Alec Guinness as Osric, Glen Byam Shaw as Laertes, John Gielgud as Hamlet, Jack Hawkins as Horatio and Laura Cowie as Gertrude in Hamlet.

NOAH – 1935

George Devine as the Bear, Harry Andrews as the Lion, Alec Guinness as the Wolf, Susan Salaman as the Lamb, Ewynn Owen as the Monkey, Merula Salaman as the Tiger and Barbara Seymour as the Cow in André Obey's Noah, *directed by Michel Saint-Denis at the New Theatre.*

JOHN GIELGUD, like many others, had been deeply impressed by the dignity and naivety of the play when it had been staged in London, four years earlier, in an enchanting French production by the *Compagnie des Quinze*. He invited its director, Michel Saint-Denis, to direct him in the title role. The English production suffered from an American translation which failed to capture the charm of the original.

ROMEO AND JULIET – 1935

Alec Guinness as the Apothecary and John Gielgud as Romeo in Shakespeare's Romeo and Juliet, *directed by John Gielgud at the New Theatre.*

THIS WAS the famous production in which John Gielgud and Laurence Olivier, in their first and last appearance together in a play, alternated Romeo and Mercutio. Peggy Ashcroft played Juliet.

There was a goodly drawing by Mr Alec Guinness of the Apothecary.
ALAN DENT *MANCHESTER GUARDIAN*

THE SEAGULL – 1936

John Gielgud as Boris Trigorin, Frederick Lloyd as Peter Sorin, Ivor Barnard as Medvedenko, George Devine as Ilya Shamrayef, Clare Harris as Paulina, Alec Guinness as a workman, Michael Brennan as Yakov, Edith Evans as Irina Arcadina, Jean Winstanley as a maid and Andrew Churchman as a cook in Anton Chekhov's The Seagull, *directed by Theodore Komisarjevsky at the New Theatre.*

THE SEAGULL was the first full-scale production of a play by Chekhov in the West End and was by common consent the highwater mark of Komisarjevsky's achievement, famous for its poetic beauty and the brilliant ensemble work of the distinguished cast.

There is no play now running worthy to be mentioned in the same breath as The Seagull.
HERBERT FARJEON *SUNDAY PICTORIAL*

LOVE'S LABOUR'S LOST – 1936

Margaretta Scott as Rosaline, Rosamund Greenwood as Katharine, Katharine Page as Maria, Rachel Kempson as the Princess of France and Alec Guinness as Boyet in Shakespeare's Love's Labour's Lost, *directed by Tyrone Guthrie at the Old Vic Theatre.*

SHAKESPEARE's affectionate parody of pedantic and romantic ostentation, was given a beautiful production by Tyrone Guthrie.

Boyet is the lord attending the Princess of France, who acts as messenger between her and the court of Navarre. In his autobiography, *Blessings in Disguise*, Guinness describes his performance as 'wretched and humourless' – an opinion not shared by Audrey Williamson, in *Old Vic Drama*, who found him 'perfect and stylish'.

AS YOU LIKE IT – 1936

Douglas Matthews as Oliver, Eileen Peel as Celia, Michael Redgrave as Orlando, Edith Evans as Rosalind, James Dale as Jaques, Ernest Hare as the Duke, Freda Jackson as Audrey, Milton Rosmer as Touchstone, John Kempson as Silvius and Daphne Heard as Phebe in Shakespeare's As You Like It, directed by Esmé Church at the Old Vic Theatre.

Edith Evans was one of the great Rosalinds. The production was dressed in the style of Watteau, and such was its success that it transferred to the New Theatre, though without Guinness who joined John Gielgud's company at the Queen's Theatre.

He played the rustic William who is in love with the sluttish Audrey. (He is standing at the back, fifth from the right.) It was a role, according to his autobiography, he loved playing. Alan Dent, critic of the *Manchester Guardian*, described his performance as 'a wondrous blank'. Guinness also played Le Beau, the affected courtier, a role he said he loathed.

HAMLET – 1937

Robert Newton as Horatio, Laurence Olivier as Hamlet and Alec Guinness as Osric in Shakespeare's Hamlet, *directed by Tyrone Guthrie at the Old Vic Theatre.*

Mr Guinness's Osric is also an admirable popinjay and wisely not effeminate.

IVOR BROWN *OBSERVER*

TWELFTH NIGHT – 1937

Jessica Tandy as Viola, Laurence Olivier as Sir Toby Belch and Alec Guinness as Sir Andrew Aguecheek in Shakespeare's Twelfth Night, *directed by Tyrone Guthrie at the Old Vic Theatre.*

IN A PRODUCTION which Guthrie himself described as baddish and immature, Guinness's comic restraint was much appreciated and admired.

There was so much tumbling and gurgling and slapping in the clowns' parts that I began to wonder why they had any text at all.
IVOR BROWN *OBSERVER*

Mr Guinness reminded me powerfully of Stan Laurel – and there's a good deal of Laurel and Hardy in Sir Andrew and Sir Toby. He sustains throughout a character of well-intentioned, almost agreeable silliness which is beautifully controlled.
J.G. BERGEL *EVENING NEWS*

RICHARD II – 1937

John Gielgud as Richard and Alec Guinness as Aumerle in Shakespeare's Richard II, *directed by John Gielgud at the Queen's Theatre.*

HENRY V – 1937

Alec Guinness as the Duke of Exeter, Laurence Olivier as Henry and Harcourt Williams as the Archbishop of Canterbury in Shakespeare's Henry V, *directed by Tyrone Guthrie at the Old Vic Theatre.*

THE SCHOOL FOR SCANDAL – 1937

Alec Guinness as Snake, Dorothy Green as Lady Sneerwell and Merula Salaman as a maid in Richard Brinsley Sheridan's The School for Scandal, *directed by Tyrone Guthrie at the Queen's Theatre.*

Guinness's malicious Snake was perfect Hogarth. Sitting there, drinking chocolate with Lady Sneerwell, gossiping, he might very easily have stepped out of the levée scene from the *Marriage à la Mode* sequence.

Guthrie's over-stylised production was thought to be something of a scandal, many critics complaining that the choreographed movement was more appropriate to a ballet than to Sheridan's play.

> *Why must Mr Alec Guinness put an inch of putty on Mr Snake's nose?*
> JAMES AGATE *SUNDAY TIMES*

THREE SISTERS – 1938

Peggy Ashcroft as Irina, Michael Redgrave as Tusenbach, Harry Andrews as Roddey, George Devine as Andrey, Glen Byam Shaw as Solyony, Frederick Lloyd as Tchebutykin, Alec Guinness as Fedotik and Carol Goodner as Masha in Anton Chekhov's Three Sisters, *directed by Michel Saint-Denis at the Queen's Theatre.*

Three sisters was one of the great Chekhovian productions of the 1930s, beautifully co-ordinated and orchestrated by Michel Saint-Denis, and much admired for its meticulous detail and the team-work of an all-star cast. For A.E. Wilson, critic of the *Star*, it was 'one of the richest experiences London has ever offered or is likely to offer'.

THE MERCHANT OF VENICE – 1938

Genevieve Jessell as Jessica and Alec Guinness as Lorenzo in Shakespeare's The Merchant of Venice, *directed by John Gielgud and Glen Byam Shaw at the Queen's Theatre.*

In the first place, there is a Lorenzo by Alec Guinness who gives reason to Jessica's truancy and lifts the final scene to an unspectacular, meditative, star-struck beauty that takes the breath away.

TIMES

TRELAWNY OF THE 'WELLS' – 1938

Sophie Stewart as Rose Trelawny, Alec Guinness as Arthur Gower and O.B. Clarence as Sir William Gower in Arthur Wing Pinero's Trelawny of the 'Wells', *directed by Tyrone Guthrie at the Old Vic Theatre.*

PINERO's unashamedly sentimental comedy recalls a major turning-point in British theatre in the 1860s when the Vincent Crummels school of acting was beginning to give way to the new naturalism of the 'cup-and-saucer' dramas of Tom Robertson, a playwright who wanted his stage characters to talk and behave like real people.

Arthur Gower marries the heroine. It's not much of a part. The audience would far rather Rose Trelawny married Tom Wrench, Pinero's affectionate portrait of Tom Robertson, and the real hero of the play.

HAMLET – 1938

Hermione Hannen as Ophelia and Alec Guinness as Hamlet in Shakespeare's Hamlet, *directed by Tyrone Guthrie at the Old Vic Theatre.*

G UTHRIE'S production was acted in its entirety and in modern dress. Guinness was twenty-four-years old.

Visually the most striking scene (and one that is still remembered to this day) was Ophelia's dreary funeral in the rain with the mourners carrying open umbrellas.

His youth, combined with rare intelligence, humour and pathos, realised a great deal of the part. He had not yet quite the authority to support, as Hamlet must, a whole evening, or to give the tragedy its full stature. The performance demanded that the public reach out and take what was offered. To this demand the public is rarely equal.
TYRONE GUTHRIE *A LIFE IN THE THEATRE*

His vital sensitive portrait shows finely balanced intelligence tortured and distorted, but never weak or neurotic. The nobility and simplicity of his acting and of his speaking is matched by the production.
BYSTANDER

Mr Guinness's Hamlet fails and non-fails. It fails because it deliberately refuses to succeed. This young actor is obviously not trying any of the things in Hamlet which are the ABC of the part. He attempts neither play of feature nor gesture. He rejects mordancy.
JAMES AGATE *SUNDAY TIMES*

I have never seen a better young Hamlet than his.
HAROLD HOBSON *OBSERVER*

I was merely a pale shadow of Gielgud with some fustian Freudian trimmings, encouraged – he will forgive me, I know – by Guthrie.
ALEC GUINNESS *SPECTATOR*

Alec Guinness as Hamlet and Malcolm Keen as the Ghost in Hamlet.

THE RIVALS – 1938

Andre Morell as Faulkland and Alec Guinness as Bob Acres in Richard Brinsley Sheridan's The Rivals, *directed by Esmé Church at the Old Vic Theatre.*

S HERIDAN'S gentle, kindly play manages to be and mock the thing it is: a sentimental comedy with a full complement of eighteenth-century stereotypes.

The very special appeal of Guinness's Bob Acres, up from country and swearing with propriety, was that he was such a likeable coward, an awkward, bashful, charming booby, and not the usual boisterous idiot.

The Bob Acres of Mr Alec Guinness is disturbingly fragile and sentient: the suffering clown.
NEW STATESMAN AND NATION

It seems to me to be a delicious performance of quite another character. He is moonstruck, not moonfaced; he has a pathos which knocks the whole comedy sideways; he is a little like a number of the young Bobs and Dicks, Mr Toots and Master Traddles in Dickens, and not in the least like Sheridan's Bob Acres. All the same, it is a fascinating performance, and I am not so very fond of Bob Acres that I deplore the wrongness.
RICHARD PRENTIS *JOHN O'LONDON'S WEEKLY*

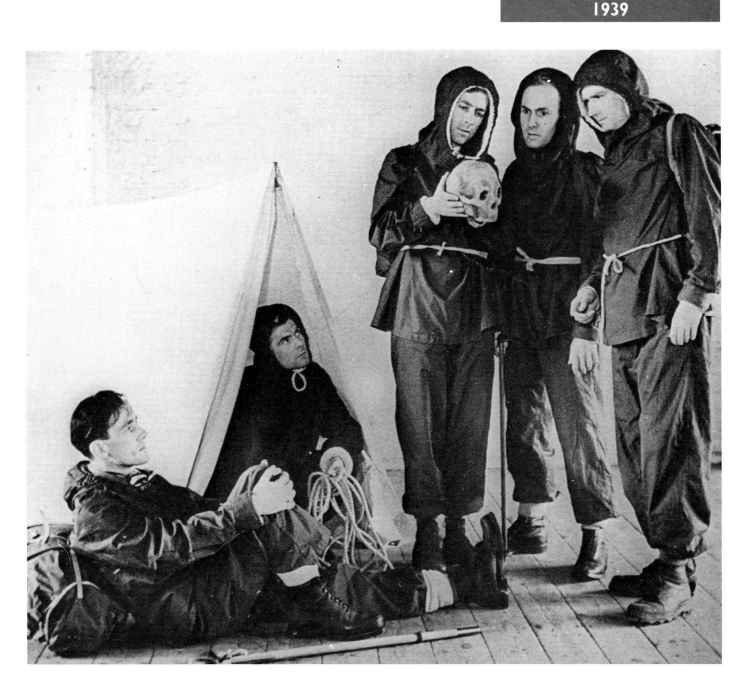

THE ASCENT OF F.6 – 1939

Alec Guinness as Michael Ransom, Frederick Peisley as Edward Lamp, Arthur Macrae as David Gunn, Laurier Lister as Ian Shawcross and Ernest Hare as Dr Williams in W.H. Auden and Christopher Isherwood's The Ascent of F.6, directed by Rupert Doone at the Old Vic Theatre.

THE ASCENT OF F.6, written in a mixture of prose and poetry, is not easy: part fairy tale, part political statement, the play describes a journey of self-discovery, leading to salvation and death on a demon-haunted mountain.

Guinness, as the leader of the expedition (originally created by William Devlin at the Mercury Theatre in 1937), emphasised the character's psychological likeness to T.E. Lawrence, a role he would play twenty-one years later in Terence Rattigan's *Ross*.

It was a fascinating performance, undoubtedly Guinness's most forceful achievement before the war.
AUDREY WILLIAMSON *THEATRE OF TWO DECADES*

Mr Alec Guinness as the leader of the fatal mountaineering expedition, delivers with judgement the poetic prose speeches. He suggests the character's grave and humorous detachment in the earlier scenes but, understandably perhaps, loses some of his control in the Freudian labyrinth in which the play finally extinguishes itself.
RICHARD CLOWES *SUNDAY TIMES*

ROMEO AND JULIET – 1939

Pamela Stanley as Juliet and Alec Guinness as Romeo in Shakespeare's Romeo and Juliet, *directed by Willard Stoker at Perth Theatre.*

GREAT EXPECTATIONS – 1939

Alec Guinness as Herbert Pocket and Marius Goring as Pip in Alec Guinness's adaptation of Charles Dickens's Great Expectations, *directed by George Devine at Rudolf Steiner Hall.*

CHARLES DICKENS said of Herbert Pocket that he had a natural incapacity to do anything secret or mean; and it was this fresh-faced, frank, buoyant quality which Guinness caught so well, and which would be preserved in David Lean's classic film seven years later.

Opposite: *Alec Guinness in* Oliver Twist *1948*

1940s

COUSIN MURIEL – 1940

Peggy Ashcroft as Dinah Sylvester and Alec Guinness as Richard Meilhac in Clemence Dane's Cousin Muriel, *directed by Norman Marshall at the Globe Theatre.*

Cousin Muriel was a liar, forger, cheat and kleptomaniac. Guinness was cast as her son, unfairly tarred with the same brush. Peggy Ashcroft played the girl he wanted to marry.

The general feeling was that Edith Evans was miscast in the title role and that the third act did not work.

THE TEMPEST – 1940

Jessica Tandy as Miranda, John Gielgud as Prospero and Alec Guinness as Ferdinand in Shakespeare's The Tempest, *directed by George Devine and Marius Goring at the Old Vic Theatre.*

Mr Alec Guinness, one of the best actors in England, was inevitably good as the tranced Ferdinand.
NEW STATESMAN AND NATION

Mr Alec Guinness is a flawlessly romantic Ferdinand.
TIMES

Mr Alec Guinness is always interesting, but surely Ferdinand is an ordinary young man bewitched and not so strange in essence.
IVOR BROWN OBSERVER

FLARE PATH – 1942

Alec Guinness as Flight Lieutenant Graham in Terence Rattigan's
Flare Path, *directed by Margaret Webster at the Henry Miller Theatre, New York.*

Rattigan's first serious play, set in wartime England on the night of an important bombing raid, did not repeat its London success on Broadway.

Guinness played a young pilot, terribly nice, very immature, married to a glamorous actress who, as part of her contribution to the war effort, gives up her lover and her career when she realises for the first time the strain her husband is under and how much he needs her.

Flare Path succeeded in London because it was about the war. It failed in New York for precisely the same reason. Lewis Nichols, critic of *The New York Times*, admired Guinness's 'nervous energy and bounce' but found the play 'sentimental, slow and confused'.

THE BROTHERS KARAMAZOV – 1946

Elizabeth Sellars as Grushenka and Alec Guinness as Mitya Karamazov in Alec Guinness's adaptation from Fydor Dostoevsky's The Brothers Karamazov, *directed by Peter Brook at the Lyric Theatre, Hammersmith.*

Despite the brilliance of Peter Brook's production and the acting (Frederick Valk as old Karamazov, in particular) there were many critics who did not think selected episodes from Dostoevsky's novel added up to a play.

Guinness played Mitya with nail-biting ardour.
KENNETH TYNAN *HE THAT PLAYS THE KING*

Mitya, the wild unhappy youth sentenced for the murder which he has aimed at but not committed, is played by Mr Guinness himself with a burning directness which over-simplified the part but certainly makes it forceful and intelligible.
ERIC KEOWN *PUNCH*

One could perhaps best describe Mr Alec Guinness's adaptation by saying that it is one of those colossal mistakes which are tremendously worth doing. . . . As Mitya Mr Alec Guinness disappointed in the first two acts, largely owing to a manner and make-up which suggested Victorian revels in a coterie theatre at the top of six flights of stairs; when he got down to bare feet and convict's garb his playing took on the required intensity.
JAMES AGATE *SUNDAY TIMES*

VICIOUS CIRCLE – 1946

*Beatrix Lehmann as Inez, Alec Guinness as Garcin and Betty Ann
Davies as Estelle in Jean-Paul Sartre's* Vicious Circle, *directed by
Peter Brook at the Arts Theatre Club.*

Hell is other people.

Vicious circle is the English title for Sartre's existen-
tialist melodrama *Huis Clos*, a legal phrase to cover the
period during which the law courts are closed for the
vacation.

 The play is about three people in hell. Hell is a
claustrophobic, windowless room, whose fierce electric light
can never be turned off; the furniture is three Second
Empire sofas.

 The central weakness is that what the three damned
souls have done is far too explicit and not that interesting.
The play's strength is their collective agony in knowing that
they are trapped together for all eternity.

 Guinness was cast as a sadistic and neurotic coward,
whose life had ended with twelve bullets through his chest.

KING LEAR – 1946

*Nicholas Hannen as the Earl of Kent, Alec Guinness as the Fool,
Laurence Olivier as Lear and Michael Warre as Edgar in
Shakespeare's* King Lear, *directed by Laurence Olivier, for the
Old Vic Company, at the New Theatre.*

*Mr Alec Guinness played the teasing, transient part which always
promises more than it yields better than I have ever seen it done before.
He disdained the fidgety, skip-and-jump method and the prancing
whimsy and gives us instead the queer, still, frightened fancy of a
whipped menial, poignant as a puppy in pain, with the finest shades
of understanding and apprehension flickering across his face.*

IVOR BROWN *OBSERVER*

*It is a part, which with its skipping and wisecracks, can be very
tedious. Few actors succeed in getting through the incongruity to the
enormous pathos behind, but Mr Guinness does this brilliantly. His
Fool is infinitely sad and infinitely humorous and for once Lear's
affection for him can be understood.*

ERIC KEOWN *PUNCH*

AN INSPECTOR CALLS – 1946

Margaret Leighton as Sheila Birling and Alec Guinness as Eric Birling in J.B. Priestley's An Inspector Calls, *directed by Basil Dean, for the Old Vic Company, at the New Theatre.*

AN INSPECTOR CALLS, now recognised as a minor classic, was under-estimated in London, though not in Moscow where it received its first performance.

The play, an Edwardian swan song and socialist tract against capitalist greed, was the best detective story theatregoers had seen since the previous season's *Oedipus Rex.*

Priestley built his drama strictly on classical lines, the tension coming entirely from the predictability of the plot in which it is gradually revealed that everybody has been responsible for a girl's suicide.

Guinness played the young man who had made her pregnant and deserted her. Philip Hope-Wallace, writing in *Time and Tide*, thought he was brilliant.

CYRANO DE BERGERAC – 1946

In the centre, Nicholas Hannen as Ragueneau, Alec Guinness as Comte de Guiche, John Arnold as a cadet and, *far right,* Ralph Richardson as Cyrano in Edmond Rostand's Cyrano de Bergerac, *directed by Tyrone Guthrie, for the Old Vic Company, at the New Theatre.*

ROSTAND, hankering after some long-lost, romantic, chivalric ideal, wrote *Cyrano de Bergerac* as an antidote to the problem plays of his own day. The result was a dazzling theatrical mixture of rhyme and rapier – a firework display of verbal and visual *panache*.

A remarkable study of de Guiche once again established Alec Guinness as an actor of outstanding quality. Looking like a portrait by Van Dyck, he brought to the man an aristocrat's distinction, impeccable style, and the suave, lean-cheeked and subtle craft of a nephew of Richelieu.

AUDREY WILLIAMSON *OLD VIC DRAMA*

GREAT EXPECTATIONS – 1946

John Mills as Pip and Alec Guinness as Herbert Pocket in the film version of Charles Dickens's Great Expectations, *directed by David Lean.*

Herbert Pocket had a frank and easy way with him that was very taking.

CHARLES DICKENS

HERBERT POCKET is Pip's unassuming companion, tutor and friend. Guinness was authentic Dickens. He might have sat for Cruikshank. He quite simply *was* Pocket, a truly delightful fellow. His innate goodness was visible for all to see.

THE ALCHEMIST – 1947

Alec Guinness as Abel Drugger in Ben Jonson's The Alchemist, *directed by John Burrell, for the Old Vic Company, at the New Theatre.*

Drugger used to be Garrick's part, but, Mr Guinness having now appropriated it, I name him the best living English character-actor.
KENNETH TYNAN *HE WHO PLAYS THE KING*

His Abel Drugger is a lisping nincompoop suggesting, with the text's authority, a wondrous blend of asinity and halitosis. This player creates (or recreates) every part he touches.
IVOR BROWN *OBSERVER*

Mr Guinness endows the tobacco-seller, for at least one spectator, with the pathos and pity of some tiny, captive monkey gambolling heartbreakingly to the full length of its chain. Or you may take the other view and, ready to tumble off your seat at clowning of such drollery, wonder what your neighbour finds to snivel at. Either way, a glorious piece of playing.
JAMES AGATE *SUNDAY TIMES*

RICHARD II – 1947

Harry Andrews as Henry Bolingbroke, Peter Copley as Thomas Mowbray and Alec Guinness as Richard in Shakespeare's Richard II, *directed by Ralph Richardson, for the Old Vic Company, at the New Theatre.*

He speaks Shakespeare beautifully and with complete understanding.
ERIC KEOWN *PUNCH*

The greatest speeches were spoken with the keenest intelligence, but with something less than magic.
IVOR BROWN *OBSERVER*

Mr Guinness is a highly intelligent actor, and brilliantly catches the mixture of the character. This, though, is a part that calls on every quality in an actor: there are in it a personal grace, a melody of speech, and a theatrical beauty for which Mr Guinness does not seem equipped.
LIONEL HALE *DAILY MAIL*

Mr Guinness's genius is for the rueful comic, a note which this play never strikes.
JAMES AGATE *SUNDAY TIMES*

Mr Guinness gives a very fine performance indeed; there is a kind of quiet, almost sly, precision about his acting which is as attractive as it is difficult to define.
SPECTATOR

SAINT JOAN – 1947

Alec Guinness as The Dauphin and Celia Johnson as Joan in Saint Joan.

Alec Guinness as The Dauphin in George Bernard Shaw's Saint Joan, directed by John Burrell, for the Old Vic Company, at the New Theatre.

Mr Alec Guinness's Dauphin is a triumph. It suggests a sharp-nosed, half-witted schoolgirl in its red stockings and its yellow smock, and it replies to all the bullying it encounters with a flouncing and sulky resentment that is endearing as well as comic.

HAROLD HOBSON SUNDAY TIMES

Alec Guinness as the Dauphin is a superb piece of shrivelled humanity, wry, caustic, disenchanted: in this kind of part Guinness is not only good for us today; I think he would have found a place with Munden in Lamb's gallery of master-drolls.

IVOR BROWN OBSERVER

THE GOVERNMENT INSPECTOR –
1948

Alec Guinness as Hlestakov in Nikolai Gogol's The Government Inspector, *directed by John Burrell, for the Old Vic Company, at the New Theatre.*

WHEN HIS SATIRE on tsarist bureaucracy was first produced in 1836, Gogol warned his actors to guard against the use of caricature. It is a warning which has gone largely unheeded in England. Feliks Topolski's grotesque costumes and heavy make-up turned the actors into marionettes.

Hlestakov is a stuck-up little clerk on the lowest grade in the civil service. While travelling in a provincial backwater, penniless and starving, he suddenly finds himself lionised and fêted, the whole town ('a cesspit of corruption') falling over itself to give him money.

Guinness, in a delightful and exquisite performance, was particularly amusing when Hlestakov gets very drunk and entertains the company with descriptions of his non-existent social whirl and intellectual success in Petersburg.

In this role Alec Guinness is immaculately funny. If his performance is Chaplinesque in its puffed-up elegance, Bernard Miles's blundering mayor is Hogarthian: the very contrast of their comedy is a joy.

CECIL WILSON *DAILY MAIL*

Alec Guinness in The Government Inspector.

CORIOLANUS – 1948

Alec Guinness as Menenius in Shakespeare's Coriolanus, *directed by E. Martin Browne, for the Old Vic Company, at the New Theatre. John Clements played Coriolanus.*

THE GENERAL consensus was that Guinness's portrait of the wise old patrician was easily the best and most moving acting in the production. Many critics felt that he had, in fact, stolen the play.

This is in some ways the best part, but I protest strongly the use of the hateful phrase, 'stealing the play,' when a good actor has a good opportunity and takes it properly. Actors who 'steal plays' should be drummed off the stage. Theft is not part of their craft, and Guinness gives a beautiful loyal performance 'in support'.

IVOR BROWN *OBSERVER*

Mr Guinness has always been a gifted character actor, though I have sometimes felt him to be too self-conscious about his own cleverness. But his Menenius is a most convincing performance and admirably subordinated to the whole design.

T.C. WORSLEY *NEW STATESMAN AND NATION*

OLIVER TWIST – 1948

Alec Guinness as Fagin and John Howard Davies as Oliver in the film version of Charles Dickens's Oliver Twist, *directed by David Lean.*

OLIVER TWIST – 1948

Alec Guinness as Fagin, Robert Newton as Bill Sikes and Kay Walsh as Nancy in the film version of Charles Dickens's Oliver Twist, *directed by David Lean.*

DAVID LEAN'S *Oliver Twist*, one of the great Dickens's adaptations (though not always appreciated as such by the critics of the day), is a masterpiece of visual story-telling, memorable for its atmospheric storm-opening, the grim realism of the workhouse, and the brilliant editing of the whole 'Please, sir, I want some more' sequence.

Guinness was practically unrecognisable in his repulsive disguise. His villainous-looking merry old gentleman was a perfect theatrical mirror to the squalor and degredation of the London slums in the 1830s.

Fagin was ingratiating, oily, playful, kindly even (to the boys at least), and comic. But there was no mistaking the danger in his mock-courteous welcome to Oliver on his recapture (*Delighted to see you looking so well, my dear*) nor in his egging Sikes to murder Nancy (*You won't be too violent, Bill. I mean not for safety*).

Guinness, true to Dickens and Cruikshank, was both frightening and frightened. The light of terror was always there in his bright dark eyes, sometimes played for comedy, sometimes for real. His trial and last night in prison were condensed into one single cry to the baying, bloodthirsty mob: *What right have you to butcher me?*

The Motion Picture Association of America banned the film for two years for alleged anti-semitism; and the ban was not lifted until some seven to ten minutes had been cut, mainly of close-ups of Guinness's face. The grotesque hooked-nose gave particular offence. There were riots by the Polish Jews in Berlin, and the film had to be withdrawn there as well.

J. Arthur Rank pointed out that if every race, profession and sect objected to the unflattering portrait of its members, there could be no fiction at all.

There is a touch of impishness as well as evil about Fagin, and I cannot imagine the scenes being better done, or indeed now, otherwise done.
WILLIAM WHITEBAIT *NEW STATESMAN AND NATION*

It is vastly clever – harsh, ugly, sly, unwholesome, yet curiously appealing.
BOSLEY CROWTHER *NEW YORK TIMES*

KIND HEARTS AND CORONETS
–1949

Alec Guinness as six members of the d'Ascoyne family and Valerie Hobson (second from left) as Edith d'Ascoyne in Kind Hearts and Coronets, *a film directed by Robert Hamer. French title:* Noblesse Oblige.

KIND HEARTS AND CORONETS, a satirical black comedy of manners, based on Roy Horniman's novel *Israel Rank*, was an immensely civilised entertainment, written, directed and acted with sophisticated wit and irony. John Dighton's screenplay, in the Oscar Wilde idiom, knowing and coolly cynical, described the efforts of a young man (Dennis Price) to gain his birthright by murdering the eight people who stood between him and the Dukedom.

Guinness played all eight characters, neat cameos and caricatures of the English aristocracy: banker, ladies' man, photographer, admiral, general, suffragette, parson and duke.

The admiral, who goes down with his sinking ship, and the suffragette, who is killed while travelling in a balloon, were cardboard cut-outs. The general, who dies telling the same old boring story (a parody of C. Aubrey Smith in *The Four Feathers*), and the ladies' man, who disappears over the weir while he is busy making love in a punt, were quick sketches.

His most rewarding roles were the kindly old banker who dies of a stroke, the likeable newly wed photographer who is blown up in his dark-room, the deaf old parson who is poisoned, and the brutal duke who is caught in one of his own man-traps and murdered in cold blood – a scene of unexpected viciousness.

The parson ('I always say that my west window has all the exuberance of Chaucer without happily any of the concomitant crudities') was the best loved of all the portraits.

Such was Guinness's success that some people thought he should have played the murderer as well.

He gives to all these varied characters such superb attack and fluency of mannerism, such a wonderful felicity of invention that he should get some kind of award for his work.
PAUL HOLT *DAILY HERALD*

Consider the artistry of Mr Alec Guinness. All London speaks well of him today. I've no doubt he'll conquer what remains of the world tomorrow.
SUNDAY DISPATCH

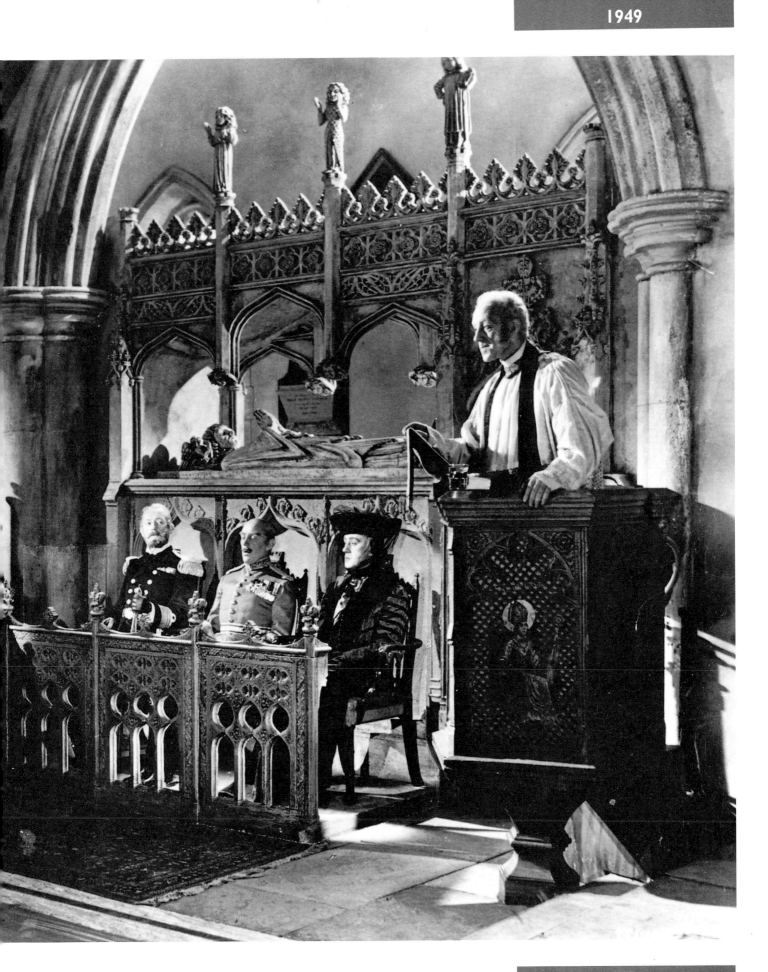

KIND HEARD AND CORONETS –
1949

Alec Guinness as all eight members of the d'Ascoyne family and
Dennis Price as Louis Mazzini in Kind Hearts and Coronets.

THE HUMAN TOUCH – 1949

Alec Guinness as Dr James Young Simpson and Sophie Stewart as Mrs Simpson in J. Lee Thompson and Dudley Leslie's The Human Touch, *directed by Peter Ashmore at the Savoy Theatre.*

JAMES YOUNG SIMPSON was the first physician to use chloroform as an anaesthetic. *The Human Touch* described his battle with the Edinburgh medical fraternity in 1847.

Guinness's charm, grace and pathos were admired but the play, poorly constructed and dull, was not.

THE COCKTAIL PARTY – 1949

Robert Flemyng as Edward Chamberlayne, Ursula Jeans as Lavinia Chamberlayne, Ernest Clark as Alexander MacColgie Gibbs, Cathleen Nesbitt as Julia Shuttlethwaite and Alec Guinness as an Unidentified Guest in T.S. Eliot's The Cocktail Party, *directed by E. Martin Browne at the Lyceum Theatre, Edinburgh.*

THE COCKTAIL PARTY takes the classical ingredients of sin, guilt and expiation, and presents them within a Christian cycle of death and re-birth.

Guinness, mysterious, remote, cryptic, whimsical, authoritative, was perfect casting for the Unidentified Guest, later identified as Sir Henry Harcourt-Reilly, a metaphysical psychologist, who offers spiritual guidance to his patients.

Critics and public alike found T.S. Eliot's drawing-room comedy difficult (after all, not everybody has seen the *Alcestis* of Euripides); but this in no way interfered with its intellectual and box-office success.

The week after – as well as the morning after – I take it to be nothing but a finely acted piece of flapdoodle.
ALAN DENT *NEWS CHRONICLE*

Mr Guinness is going to be one of our great actors. The triangle of Gielgud, Olivier, and Richardson is visibly changing into a quadrilateral.
HAROLD HOBSON *SUNDAY TIMES*

The production went to New York in 1950. London would have to wait nineteen years before they were able to see Guinness in *The Cocktail Party*.

A RUN FOR YOUR MONEY – 1949

Edward Rigby as a Beefeater and Alec Guinness as Whymple in A Run for Your Money, a film directed by Charles Frend.

Mr Guinness understands that to be really funny you have to take everything in the deadliest of earnest. He has the slow gravity, the grace and absorption of a circus elephant and I loved every minute of him.

PAUL HOLT *DAILY HERALD*

A RUN FOR YOUR MONEY fell well below the high standards Ealing Studios had set herself in *Passport to Pimlico, Whisky Galore* and *Kind Hearts and Coronets*.

Guinness was cast as the mournful gardening correspondent of the *London Echo*: a timid, prim whimp who preferred vegetables to people. He is assigned to chaperone two young Welsh miners who have won a £200 prize newspaper competition, and have come up to London for the cup.

There was a splendid shot of Guinness, sitting in the Welsh stand during the match, shouting *England!*, which was worthy of a cartoon by H.E. Bateman in his series, *The Man Who. . . .*

Opposite: *Alec Guinness in* The Ladykillers *1955*

1950s

THE COCKTAIL PARTY – 1950

Alec Guinness as Sir Henry Harcourt-Reilly and Irene Worth as Celia Coplestone in T.S. Eliot's The Cocktail Party, *directed by E. Martin Browne at the Henry Miller Theatre, New York.*

THE PRODUCTION was a smash-hit and Guinness's trenchant and dynamic playing won high praise. Brooks Atkinson, critic of *The New York Times*, thought he was superb.

Since it combined religion with psychiatry and was written by the leading poet in the English language, audiences sat before it respectfully all winter and were able simultaneously to save their souls and eavesdrop on the follies of the upper crust. No one understood the play, but everyone assumed it was important.

BROOKS ATKINSON *BROADWAY*

THE MUDLARK – 1950

Alec Guinness as Benjamin Disraeli in the film version of Theodore Bonnet's The Mudlark, *directed by Jean Negulesco.*

T HE MUDLARK was an unpopular choice for the Royal Film Performance, in some circles, mainly because it was felt that Irene Dunne, an American actress, should not be playing Queen Victoria.

The film told the story of a Thames-side waif who, in the 1870s, set his heart on seeing the old queen, a recluse for the last fifteen years.

Guinness was a shrewd and eloquent Disraeli. His finely written seven-minute speech (which he had to deliver in one take) was the high spot of the film.

The film performance of a lifetime.
C.A. LEJEUNE *OBSERVER*

It puts him in the highest category of character-actors.
MYRO *VARIETY*

The performance is a challenge to any of our younger or even older playwrights to give us a new play about Disraeli, with Mr Guinness's exquisite and impeccable creation as its ready-made star.
ALAN DENT *ILLUSTRATED LONDON NEWS*

LAST HOLIDAY – 1950

Alec Guinness as George Bird and Kay Walsh as Mrs Poole in J.B. Priestley's Last Holiday, *a film directed by Henry Cass.*

A SHY and somewhat sheepish commercial traveller is told he is suffering from a fatal disease and is given six weeks to live. He goes off to eek out his days at an expensive seaside hotel (full of British character actors behaving in a very stagey manner), where he is a great success, distributing largesse and socialism in equal measure.

Priestley's light-weight morality screenplay – hardly a film, more like a series of scenes – tirelessly plugged every irony. The surprise climax, in which it is discovered the doctor had made a terrible mistake, could be seen coming from the beginning; and the surprise double-twist that he is going to die anyway was also signalled far too early.

Guinness brought to his role of commercial traveller turned good boy scout a touch of wistful despair.

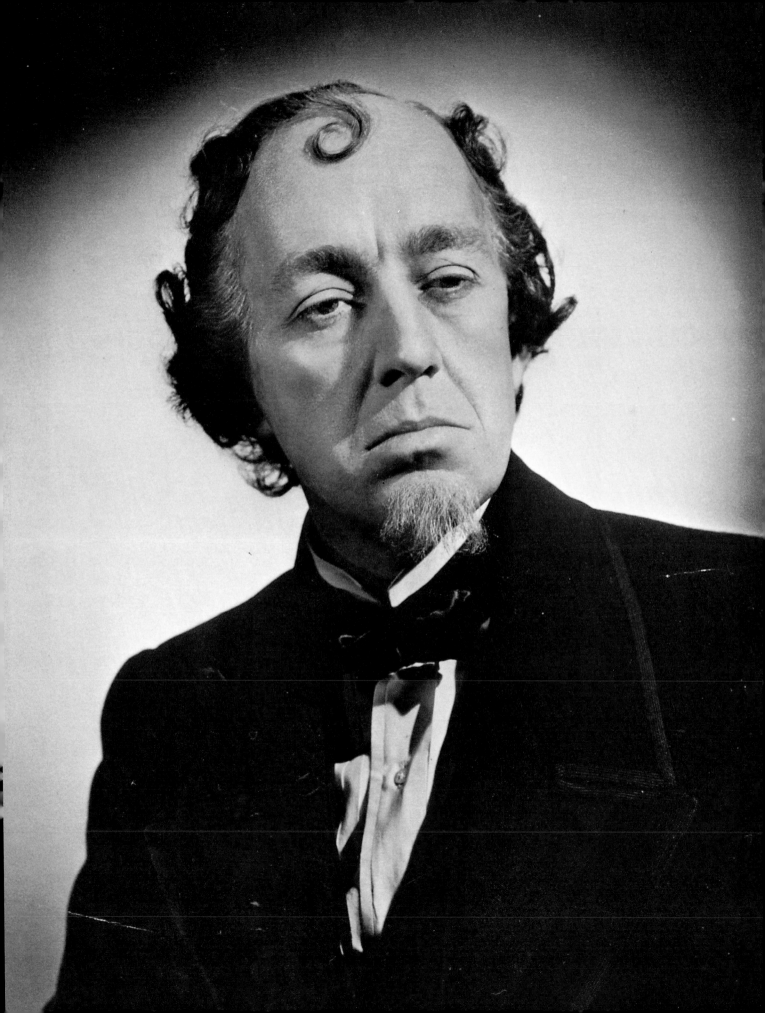

HAMLET – 1951

Alec Guinness as Hamlet, and Ken Tynan, David Spencer, Peter Wyngarde, Raymond Pike and John Weston as the Players in Shakespeare's Hamlet, *directed by Alec Guinness and Frank Hauser at the New Theatre.*

It is the custom of genius to do things in a big way, and the cropper that Mr Guinness came on Thursday night was truly monumental.
HAROLD HOBSON *SUNDAY TIMES*

This is the worst production of Hamlet *that I have ever seen.*
BEVERLEY BAXTER *EVENING STANDARD*

His bearing has no magnetism, his voice no music.
JOHN BARBER *DAILY EXPRESS*

The accepted romantic and poetic youth is nowhere; gone is the sweet Prince, and in his stead stalks a bewhiskered character, middle-aged at thirty, without passion or heart.
QUEEN

He speaks the plain text without flourish and loses thereby all romantic colour and much emotional force. On the other hand, he achieves an admirable sardonic quality which underlies and lights up everything he does, giving the performance as a whole the unmistakable stamp of individuality.
W.A. DARLINGTON *DAILY TELEGRAPH*

To the best of my ability I'm *real*. I try to follow Shakespeare's own advice to players. The critics wanted Hamlet as 'the sweet gentle prince'. He *isn't* sweet or gentle. Look at the viciousness of his colloquy with Ophelia. They wanted him young and romantic. He *isn't* all that young. He's 30. He *isn't* romantic. I don't think Shakespeare meant him to be. That is a false tradition.
ALEC GUINNESS QUOTED BY JOHN GODLEY

THE LAVENDER HILL MOB – 1951

Sidney James as Lackery, Alec Guinness as Holland and Alfie Bass as Shortie in T.E.B. Clarke's The Lavender Hill Mob, *a film directed by Charles Crichton.*

THE LAVENDER HILL MOB is, perhaps, the best loved of all Ealing Comedies. T.E.B. Clarke's original screenplay, a delightful spoof robbery film, draws freely and wittily on incidents, locations and even footage from his own seminal *The Blue Lamp*.

Guinness was cast as a meek, bowler-hatted, bespectacled Bank of England clerk, a deferential old fusspot, who supervises the delivery of bullion from the refinery to the Bank. With the help of an artist-friend he steals the bullion, converts it into souvenir models of the Eiffel Tower and exports it to France.

There was real pleasure to be had in watching him ironically accepting his supervisor's admonishment to make the most of his opportunities. Guinness brought to his role of suburban nonentity turned master-criminal, a schoolboy pride and innocent naughtiness. He and Stanley Holloway were the perfect double-act.

Stanley Holloway as Pendlebury and Alec Guinness as Holland in The Lavender Hill Mob.

THE MAN IN THE WHITE SUIT –
1951

Alec Guinness as Sidney Stratton and Joan Greenwood as Daphne Birnley in Roger Macdougall's The Man in the White Suit, *a film directed by Alexander Mackendrick.*

THE MAN IN THE WHITE SUIT, one of the very best films to come out of Ealing Studios, was a witty satire on British management in the immediate post-war years.

An ambitious young scientist invents a new kind of cloth, an artificial and unbreakable fibre which never gets dirty and lasts for ever. The invention produces a crisis in the textile industry and he is offered a quarter of a million to suppress it.

Guinness, in his luminous white suit (that suit looked as if it was wearing him) acted with a dogged Buster Keaton-like determination which was enormously appealing – funny, touching, and finally tragi-comic.

There was something heroic about the way Sidney Stratton sought out new laboratories to blow up. The apparatus he used was a star in its own right, worthy of Heath Robinson, and the gurgling, bubbling liquid and writhing tubes were splendidly orchestrated to provide a catchy signature tune which proved nearly as popular as the Harry Lime zither theme from *The Third Man*.

The Man in the White Suit was essentially serious, and the final sequence, in which Sidney is chased by an angry mob until he is cornered in a cul-de-sac and his disintegrating suit plucked from him like feathers from a chicken, was particularly nasty.

No one except Chaplin can suggest the tragi-comic better than Guinness. His part is another personal success.
STAR

Alec Guinness as Sidney Stratton in the final sequence of The Man in the White Suit.

UNDER THE SYCAMORE TREE –
1952

Alec Guinness as the Scientist in Sam and Bella Spewack's Under the Sycamore Tree, *directed by Peter Glenville at the Aldwych Theatre.*

S AM SPEWACK's farcical fable was set in an ant colony (designed by Oliver Messel) where through the brilliance of the chief ant scientist, the ants were able to share the benefits of man without enduring his hardships.

Older playgoers remembered a 1920s expressionistic satire called *The Insect Play* by the Brothers Căpek; much older playgoers remembered the birds, wasps and frogs of Aristophanes, and found the present charade tame.

Guinness's role was really a number of revue turns in which he was seen as scientist, Harley Street doctor, engineer, psychiatrist, Prince Consort, drooling father and doddering elder statesman dreaming of ways to abolish war.

He is like Beethoven spinning endless pregnant, caustic, comic, soul-searching variations on a tiny bland waltz of Diabelli which apparently had hardly anything to say in the first place.
ALAN DENT *NEWS CHRONICLE*

Looking, as always, like a slightly tipsy monk, he plays the Ant Scientist with rubber-soled charm, mincing stealth, and unfailing wit.
KENNETH TYNAN *EVENING STANDARD*

It is a mark of the extremely magnetic quality of Mr Guinness's playing that slight and even cheap though the situations and lines may sometimes seem, he can disclose a lightly veiled, sly pathos underlying the performance which brings a sudden catch in our laughing. It is beautiful acting.
PHILIP HOPE-WALLACE *MANCHESTER GUARDIAN*

THE CARD – 1952

Alec Guinness as Edward Henry ('Denry') Machin and George Devine as Mr Calvert in the film version of Arnold Bennett's The Card, *directed by Ronald Neame. US title:* The Promoter.

T HE CARD is a picaresque tale about a poor washerwoman's son who, with a bit of luck, some good ideas and a lot of cheek, becomes the youngest mayor of Brinsley. The tale is so picaresque that it seems as if Arnold Bennett is making it up as he goes along.

Guinness, the least extrovert of actors, would not have been many people's first choice for 'the most prodigious card ever born into the Five Towns'. For one thing, he lacked the North Country brashness; and for another, he never seemed to be living up to everybody's exaggerated notion of Denry.

However, on his own more modest, less vulgar, Guinness terms, he was immensely likeable. The comedy, the timing of lines and business, was a joy to watch.

He is the only comedian in films today (with the exception of Chaplin) who can conjure a laugh out of the air with a curl of his finger, a twitch of his face, or a flick of his foot.
LEONARD MOSLEY *DAILY EXPRESS*

ALL'S WELL THAT ENDS WELL –
1953

Alec Guinness as the King of France in Shakespeare's All's Well That Ends Well, *directed by Tyrone Guthrie at the Shakespeare Playhouse, Stratford-upon-Avon, Ontario.*

TYRONE GUTHRIE's elegant modern-dress production opened the Shakespeare Playhouse's very first season.
Guinness was cast in the comparatively small role of the sick king. He spent the evening in a wheelchair until Helena effected her cure – her triumph celebrated by their enchanting dancing entrance.
His performance was much admired for its grace, wit and command.

RICHARD III – 1953

Alec Guinness as Richard in Shakespeare's Richard III, *directed by Tyrone Guthrie at the Shakespeare Playhouse, Stratford-upon-Avon, Ontario.*

For Mr Guinness is a brilliant comedian, and he plays the first two acts in a light, witty key of subtle persiflage. He omits the malignancy of a notoriously revolting character. On these terms his performance is frequently amusing, but at the expense of Shakespeare's character and drama.

BROOKS ATKINSON *THE NEW YORK TIMES*

MALTA STORY – 1953

Jack Hawkins as Air Officer Commanding, Alec Guinness as Peter Ross and Anthony Steel as Bartlett in William Fairchild and Nigel Balchin's Malta Story, *a film directed by Brian Desmond Hurst.*

Malta story was a well-meaning tribute to Malta under seige in 1942, written, directed and acted with that deadening understatement so characteristic of British war films of the period.

Guinness was cast as a photographic reconnaisance pilot, an archeologist in civilian life, who falls in love with a Maltese girl before he is sent off to certain death by his stalwart and caring commanding officer.

Guinness acted the romance and heroism in the quiet, even bemused, knowledge that he was going to die at the end of the picture. His last words, as the enemy closed in for the kill ('This is where it gets tricky'), seemed almost to parody the genre.

Mr Guinness who is blessed with a rare gift for comedy seems quite lost in the banal.
VIRGINIA GRAHAM *SPECTATOR*

THE CAPTAIN'S PARADISE – 1953

Alec Guinness as Captain Henry St James, Celia Johnson as Maud and Charles Goldner as Chief Officer Rico in Alec Coppel and Nicholas Phipps's The Captain's Paradise, *a film directed by Anthony Kimmins.*

The captain's paradise was a mildly amusing anecdote about a skipper of a ferry-steamer, plying between Gibraltar and North Africa, who has a wife in both ports.

Life on the Rock was cosy domesticity, home-cooking and early to bed – a world of porridge, rissoles and cocoa. Life across the Mediterranean was more romantic, pleasure-loving and bottom-slapping – a world of champagne, flowers, and night clubs. The captain's paradise came to a predictable close when both wives, hankering after the life the other led, walked out on him.

The situation was always much better than the script. Celia Johnson, as the sensible English wife, had the best role. Guinness's funniest moment came when he was accused of being old. 'It may interest you to know, I am not fifty-three.' It was the totally humourless way he said it which was so amusing.

In the American edition of the film, in order to satisfy the demands of the censor, the captain ceased to be a bigamist and became an adulterer.

In picture after picture he is unfurled as a symbol of middle-class revolt against respectability and the law. His placid, retiring Anglo-Saxon features have become almost a gesture of defiance.
MILTON SHULMAN *EVENING STANDARD*

Yvonne de Carlo as Nita and Alec Guinness as Captain Henry St James in The Captain's Paradise.

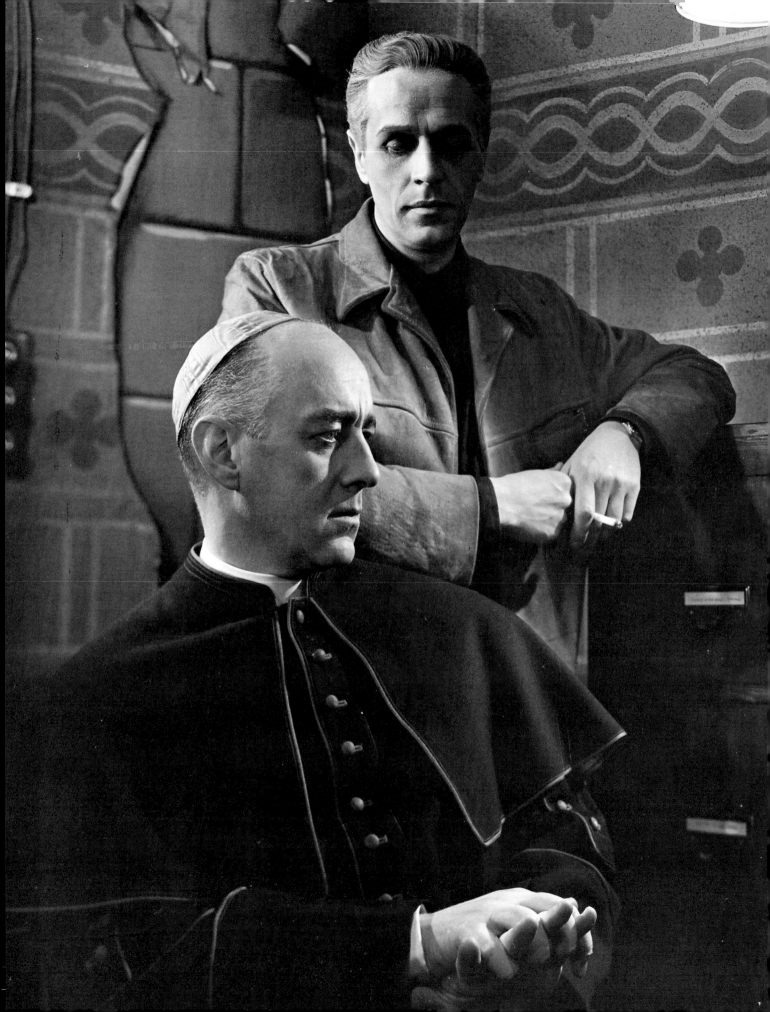

THE PRISONER – 1954

Alec Guinness as the Prisoner and Noel Willman as the Interrogator in Bridget Boland's The Prisoner, *directed by Peter Glenville at the Globe Theatre.*

Surely, it's a confession you are after, not the truth?

BRIDGET BOLAND's timely and disturbing drama, a duel of wits between the Roman Catholic Church and the Communist Party, clearly had its roots in the then recent trials of Cardinal Midszenty of Hungary and Cardinal Stepinac of Yugoslavia.

The play is set in an un-named East European totalitarian state. A much-loved cardinal, a wartime hero of the Resistance, a symbol of hope to a repressed people, is arrested on a false charge of treason. The interrogator's task is 'to deface the national monument' by extorting a public confession, thus discrediting man and church.

The interrogator succeeds after weeks of psychological torture when he discovers the cardinal's fatal flaw: namely that he had been ashamed of his mother, a prostitute, and had entered the priesthood, not from a sense of vocation but out of pride and a desire to cleanse himself. The play, and its subject matter, really deserved something better than this Freudian conclusion.

Guinness skilfully charted the prisoner's physical and mental deterioration. In a performance of power and great integrity, he revealed not only the cardinal's despair but also his arrogance and lack of humanity.

Guinness's voice throughout has a dry precision as satisfying as the music of Bach. The wonder is to see him burn up before our eyes.
JOHN BARBER *DAILY EXPRESS*

I longed for Arthur Koestler or Dostoevsky to take a hand. But Mr Guinness's study of the prisoner held me right to the end; there were gestures of fatigue acted here, which one has seen a thousand times in real life but seldom, consciously, on the stage. Such is the mark of transcendant genius in acting.
PHILIP HOPE-WALLACE *TIME AND TIDE*

Wilfrid Lawson as the Cell Warder and Alec Guinness as the Prisoner in The Prisoner.

FATHER BROWN – 1954

Alec Guinness as Father Brown and Joan Greenwood as Lady Warren in Father Brown, *a film directed by Robert Hamer. U.S. title:* The Detective.

In Father Brown, it was the chief feature to be featureless. The point about him was to appear pointless; and one might say that his conspicuous quality was not being conspicuous.
G.K. CHESTERTON

Father brown had more in common with Ealing Comedy than it did with *The Blue Cross*, the opening story in *The Innocence of Father Brown*, which had given the film its starting-point. The humour was so mild and delicate as to be almost dull; the pace so gentle and slow as to be without any suspense. The original stories are far more murderous.

Father Brown is a religious thriller in which the catching of the criminal and the return of the priceless cross of St Augustus is secondary to the saving of the criminal's soul.

Flambeau, a colossus of crime, a Gascon of gigantic stature and fantastic physical strength, was played by Peter Finch as a suave and somewhat effete aristocrat. Perhaps the nicest moment was on a train when he and Father Brown were swapping Biblical quotations in much the same way that other men might play cards.

Guinness, who could quite easily have played Chesterton's whimsical amateur detective, was asked instead to act a comic myopic version of him. He did so with compassion and saintliness.

But the picture confirms a suspicion aroused by several recent pictures; Mr Guinness is no chameleon, as first suggested by Kind Hearts and Coronets. *He is forever Guinness – good as that may be.*
JYMPSON HARMAN EVENING NEWS

Alec Guinness is a small-part player forced into stardom . . . He is precise, divine, compassionate – and arid . . . He is, in the last resort, a little man blown up beyond his true proportions.
ROBERT OTTAWAY SUNDAY GRAPHIC

TO PARIS WITH LOVE – 1955

Alec Guinness as Colonel Sir Edgar Fraser, Claude Romain as George Duprez and Vernon Gray as Jon Fraser in Robert Buckner's To Paris With Love, a film directed by Robert Hamer.

A SCOTTISH LORD takes his undergraduate son to Paris to teach him the facts of life. The boy lands a mature woman, while the father ends up with a twenty-year-old.

To Paris With Love was an old-fashioned bedroom farce; and though the sight of Guinness, with his braces caught in a hotel bedroom door or enmeshed in a badminton net, might be amusing, most critics thought he was worthy of something better.

The performance of Mr Guinness is perhaps the most pallid and listless he has ever turned in.
BOSLEY CROWTHER *THE NEW YORK TIMES*

The dry, wistful drollery of Alec Guinness is starved of opportunity.
FRED MAJDALANY *DAILY MAIL*

Forced by the script to declare his love for a 20-year-old shop assistant (Odile Versois) he yet fails to give the remotest indication that there is any more love for her in his heart than you would find on an East Coast fishmonger's slab.
W.D. ROM *EVENING STANDARD*

THE PRISONER – 1955

Jack Hawkins as the Interrogator and Alec Guinness as the Cardinal in Bridget Boland's The Prisoner, *a film directed by Peter Glenville.*

Banned as anti-Communist at the Venice Film Festival, banned by the Italian Film Board as anti-Catholic, banned in Ireland for being subtly pro-Communist, and withdrawn from the Cannes Film Festival for being politically dangerous, *The Prisoner* was clearly all things to all men.

The film could not help but be a photographed play, but the efforts, however, to get outside the interrogation room and cell were a mistake. The street scenes in particular were very contrived. The inclusion of a half-hearted love-affair was also totally expendable.

The film merely emphasised the artificial theatricality of the dialogue. The scene, for instance, where the cardinal has no difficulty in turning the tables on his persecutors and exposing their evidence as fabrications, was very glib.

The picture is a record of Guinness's stage performance. He had a new interrogator, friendlier than Noel Willman who had created the role on the London stage. Jack Hawkins's natural warmth and expansiveness was an admirable foil for Guinness's cold austerity. The two actors were well matched.

This is a film which every devout Catholic should see.
CARDINAL GRIFFIN

Alec Guinness (who plays the Cardinal) is not naturally a moving actor: precise, composed, sly, petulant, ascetic, his expression of feeling is inclined to be from the head rather than the heart. This time these particular qualities seem to be just what was wanted and within the context of the film I found him very moving indeed.
FRED MAJDALANY *TIME AND TIDE*

THE LADYKILLERS – 1955

Alec Guinness as the Professor, Katie Johnson as Mrs Wilberforce, Peter Sellers as Harry and Danny Green as One-Round in William Rose's The Ladykillers, *a film directed by Alexander Mackendrick.*

WILLIAM ROSE's brilliant black comedy (under-rated by the critics but not the public) is the story of a perfect robbery foiled by a Mrs Wilberforce, a sweet little old lady in lavender, who lives in a quaint, lopsided house, full of Edwardian bric-a-brac, which the crooks have made their headquarters, while masquerading as an amateur string quartet.

Guinness was cast as Professor Marcus, the master-mind behind an operation he had dreamt up in the booby hatch. With his protruding teeth, grey lank hair, wild eyes, hollow laughter, ghoulish grin, vulture-like shoulders, and long scarf, he presented a farcically frightening figure. He looked like a caricature of Alistair Sim as he might have been painted by Otto Dix.

Eighty-seven-year-old Katie Johnson won the British Film Academy Award for the best actress for her delightful performance as the vague yet formidably resolute Mrs Wilberforce who treats the gang as if they are all naughty boys.

Where else in the world today is there a film actor to equal the range of Alec Guinness?

JULIAN LYNNE *TRIBUNE*

The acting is triumphant. As the Professor-brains of the conspirators – I will make the claim high – the best of his comic performances I have seen: shabby-sinister, teetering on the edge of mania, yet in its lightning changes from urbane to savage cunning gloriously funny.

DILYS POWELL *SUNDAY TIMES*

Overleaf: *Alec Guinness as the Professor and Danny Green as One-Round in* The Ladykillers.

THE SWAN – 1956

Grace Kelly as Princess Alexandra and Alex Guinness as Prince Albert in the film version of Ferenc Molnar's The Swan, *directed by Charles Vidor.*

MOLNAR'S romantic comedy, mildly satirical, mildly lyrical, is an elegant theatrical trifle. A princess falls in love with her young brother's handsome tutor, and then uses him as a decoy to catch the Crown Prince, who is so bored with the task of having to choose a wife that he constantly humiliates her.

The nicest thing about Molnar's sophisticated fairy tale is the way it denies the audience's expectations. The princess marries the prince and not the tutor; and it is the tutor who is hurt and not she.

Guinness, making his Hollywood debut, played the prince with wry wit and casual charm.

Grace Kelly was the loveliest of swans. The film was released to coincide with her own royal wedding to Prince Rainier of Monaco.

HOTEL PARADISO – 1956

Irene Worth as Marcelle Cot and Alec Guinness as Boniface in Georges Feydeau and Maurice Desvallières's Hotel Paradiso, *directed by Peter Glenville at the Winter Garden Theatre.*

HOTEL PARADISO was London's first introduction to the farces of Feydeau. The production's enormous success would lead to the French bringing over their own productions and the National Theatre inviting Jacques Charon, of the Comedie Française, to stage *La Puce à L'Oreille* in English.

Guinness (in a performance notable for its physical dexterity) played Boniface, a meek and down-trodden husband who decides, in his wife's absence, to go off to a shady hotel with Mme Cot, the wife of his best friend. They never get to bed.

They find themselves spending the first part of the evening entertaining four chattering schoolgirls to tea. In the second part there is a police raid and they are arrested. Asked for their names, Boniface, with great presence of mind, tells the inspector he is Cot, just as Mme Cot, with equal presence of mind, is telling him that she is Mme Boniface.

Peter Glenville directed the play at a tremendous pace.

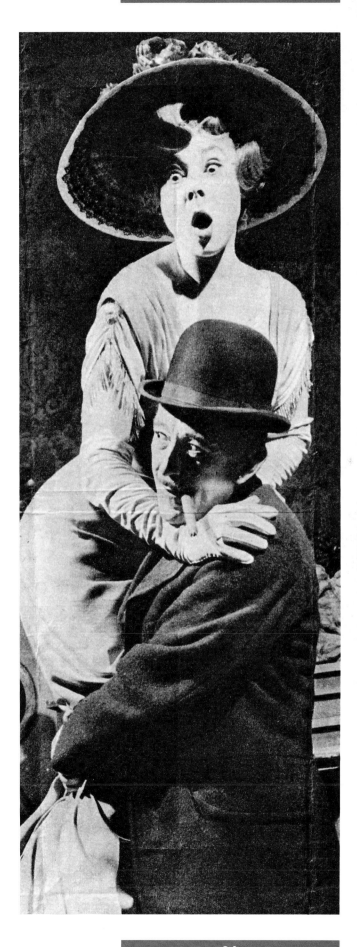

THE BRIDGE ON THE RIVER KWAI
– 1957

Alec Guinness as Colonel Nicholson in the film version of Pierre Boulle's The Bridge on the River Kwai, *directed by David Lean.*

So identified is Guinness with the role of the mad colonel that it comes as a shock to learn that not only was he not David Lean's first choice – Charles Laughton and Noël Coward were preferred – but that he himself initially turned down the part three times, convinced he could not make it work.

In Pierre Boulle's novel the bridge is left standing. In the film, inevitably, it is blown up to provide a spectacular climax. The success of the film, however, lies not in the commando raid, which is pretty boring except for the final sequence when it looks as if the colonel himself is going to stop the bridge being destroyed. The success lies rather in the scenes in the POW camp and the confrontation between the colonel and the Japanese camp commander.

The colonel agrees to build the bridge for the Japanese because he sees the operation as an exercise in morale-boosting and discipline; and also as a symbol of British supremacy. He is totally blind to the fact that he is collaborating with the enemy.

In this most difficult of roles, part hero, part fool, proud, brave, inflexible, fanatically obsessed, Guinness never lost the audience's sympathy. The film was a major turning-point in his career. With *The Bridge on the River Kwai* he became an international star.

The astonishing Alec Guinness has done it again. He steps up this week to the peak of an extraordinary career and becomes the greatest actor I have ever seen on the screen.
ANTHONY CARTHEW *DAILY HERALD*

He gives one of the most devastating portraits of a militarist that we have ever seen.
BOSLEY CROWTHER *THE NEW YORK TIMES*

Overleaf: Alec Guinness as Colonel Nicholson and Sessue Hayakawa as Colonel Saito in The Bridge on the River Kwai.

BARNACLE BILL – 1957

Irene Browne as Mrs Barrington and Alec Guinness as William Horatio Ambrose in T.E.B. Clarke's Barnacle Bill, a film directed by Charles Frend. U.S. title: All at Sea.

ONLY EALING STUDIOS could have made a film like *Barnacle Bill*, but it was a pale imitation of all that had gone before, drawing too freely on a whimsical comic mine which had long since been exhausted.

Guinness played a queasy sea captain, the last of a long line of naval heroes, who thwarts a town council's attempts to destroy a derelict Victorian pier by buying it, registering it under some Ruritanian flag, and running it like a luxury liner.

Whatever Alec Guinness had done in other funny films, he does again in this one but with the unenthusiastic, somewhat timorous air of a man who has to walk a gangplank for his living.
MILTON SHULMAN *SUNDAY EXPRESS*

But like a good captain he goes down with the script.
PHILIP OAKES *EVENING STANDARD*

To me the man is a genius. I know of nobody who in gait, eye lift and shrug can so eloquently suggest the comedy of the moment.
IVOR ADAMS *STAR*

THE HORSE'S MOUTH – 1958

Kay Walsh as Coker and Alec Guinness as Gulley Jimson in Alec Guinness's adaptation of The Horse's Mouth, *a film directed by Ronald Neame.*

GUINNESS, stubble-bearded, gravel-voiced, gave one of his finest, grittiest performances as the God-fearing atheist, Gulley Jimson, rogue, thief, sponger, crackpot, and painter of genius. Gulley refuses to conform, stripping and wrecking the flats of his wealthy patrons in his constant search for newer and bigger walls to carry his final master-piece, *The Raising of Lazarus*.

The character was always more interesting than the farce he found himself in. The savage, anarchic urge to create (*I saw a new world – a world of colour*) and the constant failure (*Not what I meant – not the vision I had*) had a beligerent grandeur, in no way diminished by a shuffling comic walk to a jaunty tune by Prokofiev.

There were two memorable visual images of Gulley. The first was when he approached his finished mural, caped in an eiderdown, looking like a bishop about to consecrate a holy work of art. The second was right at the end of the picture when he was sailing down the Thames, Tower Bridge opening like a door of a crematorium furnace, and as he passed a huge ship, he measured his thumb against the side of her vast hulk, finding, perhaps, at long last, a canvas big enough for his masterpiece.

Guinness won the Venice Film Festival Award for the best actor, and his screenplay was nominated for an 'Oscar'. *The Horse's Mouth* deserves to be much better known. Its rehabilitation is long over-due.

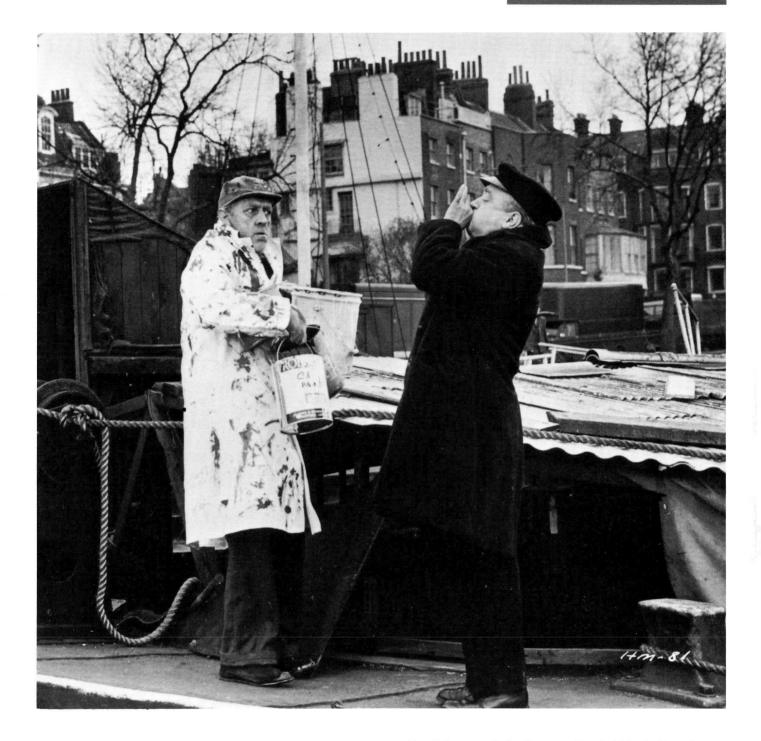

Everything is here in essence except the rage, except the tragic passion which could give solidity to the comedy. What Alec Guinness has in fact done is to make The Horse's Mouth *an intellectual Ealing-type film in which the artist, everlastingly sloshes paint on vacant white spaces, becomes the comic gimmick. And somehow one doesn't put profound faith in a gimmick.*

DILYS POWELL *SUNDAY TIMES*

Alec Guinness as Gulley Jimson and Reginald Beckwith as Captain Jones in The Horse's Mouth.

The Horse's Mouth is a great, chugging, open-handed paean to life. I fear that we have been unable to put that across on film, through our limitations, not through Joyce Cary's. My hope is that some of Cary's enthusiasm, in this unenthusiastic age, has reached the screen, and the steam, if it is there at all, will still have the property of scalding.

ALEC GUINNESS OBSERVER

THE SCAPEGOAT – 1959

Alec Guinness as John Barratt and Count Jacques de Gue in the film version of Daphne du Maurier's The Scapegoat, *directed by Robert Hamer.*

A<small>N ENGLISH DON</small>, while holidaying abroad, is tricked into changing places with his double, an unscrupulous French count. He acquires a neurotic wife, an introspective daughter, an embittered sister, a beautiful mistress, and a drug-addicted mother.

Guinness played both men with his customary precision, but was defeated by the wild improbabilities of the plot which ended with the don murdering the count. The script might have worked better had it been conceived as high comedy rather than melodrama.

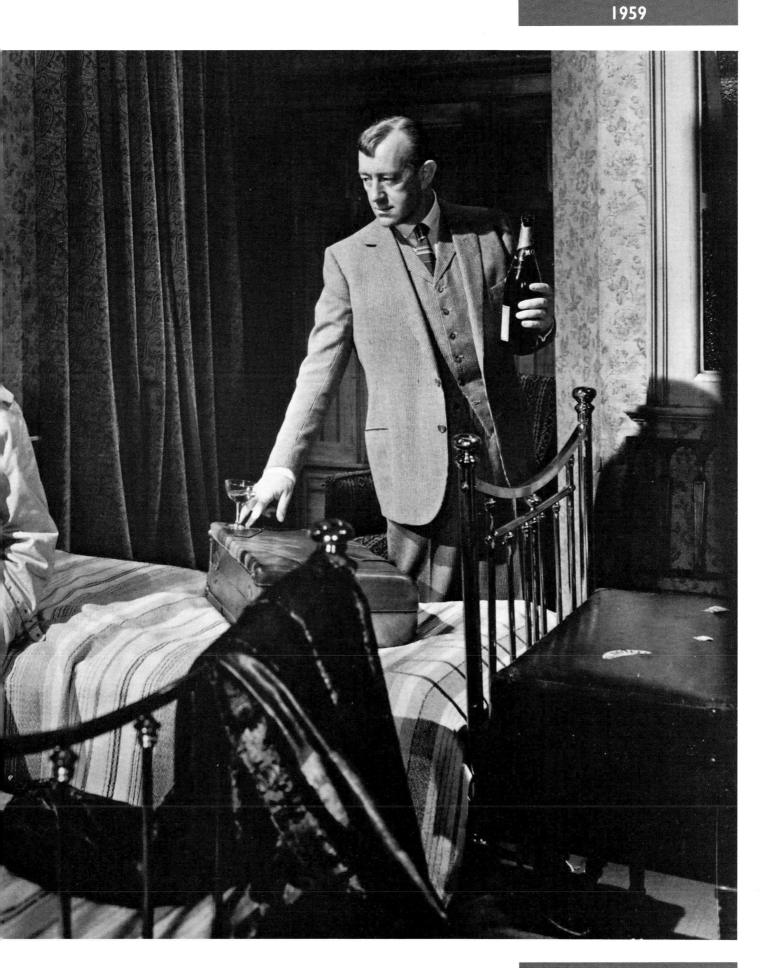

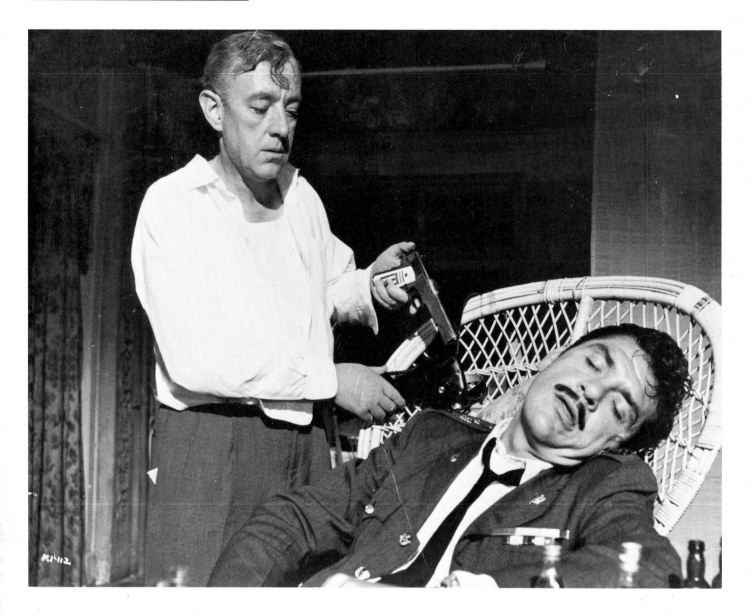

OUR MAN IN HAVANA – 1959

Alec Guinness as Jim Wormold and Ernie Kovacs as Segura in Graham Greene's Our Man in Havana, *a film directed by Carol Reed.*

GRAHAM GREENE's entertainment told the story of a vacuum cleaner salesman who allows himself to be inveigled into spying. However, since he has no vocation for the job, he simply invents agents, picking their names from the register of an exclusive club. He also supplies drawings of secret weapons, which are in fact merely drawings of giant vacuum cleaners. He deceives Whitehall; he also deceives Havana, and so convincingly that what had begun in comic fantasy ends in tragedy with people actually getting killed and he himself doing the killing.

The business lunch, where he is to speak and where he expects to be poisoned at any minute by fellow-guests and waiters, paid homage to Hitchcock. There was also an amusing scene in which Noël Coward (in his role of homburg-hatted, city-suited, furled-umbrella'd secret serviceman) tells a shocked Wormold, as if it were the most everyday thing in the world, that he is going to be murdered.

Elsewhere the film was slackly directed and Guinness came in for a great deal of adverse criticism, much of it unfair.

He glides through the picture, colourless, ordinary, negative – a ghost of the Guinness of previous films.
ANTHONY CARTHEW *DAILY HERALD*

I think, that Guinness should make a New Year's Resolution not to play any more of those mild, ordinary chaps to whom extraordinary things happen. At least not for a while.
ROY NASH *STAR*

Opposite: *Alec Guinness in* Macbeth *1966*

1960s

ROSS – 1960

Leon Sinden as Colonel Barrington, Anthony Nicholls as Ronald Storrs, Harry Andrews as General Allenby, Alec Guinness as T.E. Lawrence, Ian Clark as A.D.C. and James Grout as Franks in Terence Rattigan's Ross, directed by Glen Byam Shaw at the Theatre Royal, Haymarket.

Oh, Ross, how did I become you?

Ross acts at first like some discarded film script in which the location scenes have been left out. The play, far from being the dramatic portrait of T.E. Lawrence Rattigan had intended, is much nearer to an illustrated lecturette.

The question asked is why the legendary figure of the Middle East, the charismatic 'toff of the desert', sought anonymity in the ranks of the RAF. Two possible reasons are offered: the deaths of the Arab bodyguards he loved, and his rape by the Turkish military governor's henchmen (though you would have had to have read Lawrence's *The Seven Pillars of Wisdom* to fully appreciate the latter).

Guinness, looking remarkably like photographs of Lawrence, matched Rattigan's emotional reticence, acting with quiet authority, dry wit, and understated pathos. The scenes with General Allenby were particularly effective. His telephone call to HQ, telling them he had taken Akaba, made for an exhilarating first act curtain. But inevitably he could not bring to *Ross* more than was actually there.

Sir Alec Guinness was the only possible choice for this strange, contradictory ascetic, and his performance is as fine as sand and burned as clean.
BERNARD LEVIN DAILY EXPRESS

Sir Alec Guinness is so exactly Lawrence, in his irony, arrogance, deep sensibility, and sombre withdrawal, that we cannot conceive of an alternative reading, though there are sure to be many.
J.C. TREWIN ILLUSTRATED LONDON NEWS

There is no single moment of his performance which is not both calculated and intelligent. Somehow, however, the calculation is too apparent. He is neither Lawrence, nor Ross, nor Shaw, but an outstanding actor keeping a little aloof from the legend which he impersonates.
ALAN PRYCE-JONES OBSERVER

TUNES OF GLORY – 1960

Gordon Jackson as Captain Jimmy Cairns, John Mills as Lt Colonel Basil Barrow, Alec Guinness as Lt Colonel Jock Sinclair, Gerald Harper as Major Hugo MacMillan and Allan Cuthbertson as Captain Eric Simpson in James Kennaway's Tunes of Glory, a film directed by Ronald Neame.

Tunes of glory, a story of military honour in the officers' mess in Scotland in peace-time, offered Guinness one of his finest parts. He played an ex-piper, born in the Glaswegian slums, who had risen through the ranks to become the acting-colonel of his regiment.

Coarse-tongued, hard-drinking, loose-living, and with a temper to match his ginger hair, Jock Sinclair deeply resents the arrival of the new batallion commander, Basil Barrow, a strict disciplinarian, a product of Eton, Sand-hurst, Whitehall, whom he dismisses as 'a toy soldier' and whose authority he persistently tries to undermine.

The interesting thing about James Kennaway's screen-play was the way the audience's sympathies shifted away from Sinclair to Barrow.

The story built to a melodramatic climax in which both men cracked up, Barrow committing suicide, and Sinclair going out of his mind while addressing his brother officers on the funeral arrangements. This final difficult scene, not unreminiscent of the banquet in *Macbeth*, was acted with considerable skill.

Duncan Macrae as Pipe Major MacLean, Alec Guinness as Lt Colonel Jock Sinclair and Susannah York as Morag in Tunes of Glory.

A MAJORITY OF ONE – 1961

Rosalind Russell as Mrs Jacoby and Alec Guinness as Koichi Asano in the film version of Leonard Spigelgass's A Majority of One, directed by Mervyn LeRoy.

Sir Alec Guinness is a master of facial disguise. But in this film he has been made up to look like Alec Guinness. This is, to say the least, inappropriate to his role as a Japanese millionaire.

THOMAS WISEMAN *SUNDAY EXPRESS*

THE FILM, based on a successful Broadway play, was a plea for universal goodwill, and described the blossoming friendship of an American Jewish widow who had lost her son in the Pacific War and a Japanese Buddhist widower who had lost his daughter at Hiroshima.

It was one of those occasions when many people felt it would have been better if East and West had never met. *The Harvard Lampoon* awarded the film its 1961 OK-Doc-Break-the-Arm-Again Award for miscasting.

H.M.S. DEFIANT – 1962

Dirk Bogarde as Lieutenant Scott-Padget and Alec Guinness as Captain Crawford in HMS Defiant, *a film directed by Lewis Gilbert. U.S. title:* Damn the Defiant.

THE FILM was a schoolboy yarn in the Captain Marryat and C.S. Forester tradition, providing such popular ingredients as floggings, maggoty cheese, mutiny and gory battles.

Guinness played the captain of a frigate on escort duty during the Napoleonic wars. He was a thoroughly decent, humane sort of chap who never went above two dozen lashes, unlike his sadistic lieutenant who favoured six dozen.

He addressed the mutineers in much the same tones he had used in *The Bridge on the River Kwai*, appealing to the men's patriotism. Having won them over at an unbelievable speed, he then spoke like Lord Jervis (*We'll fight, my lads, we'll fight as if all England were watching us*) and went on to fight like Lord Nelson, losing an arm.

What these two actors saw in their parts, goodness knows.
PATRICK GIBBS *DAILY TELEGRAPH*

It is rather the sort of film one could imagine being screened before the morning runs every day at Gordonstoun.
PENELOPE GILLIATT *OBSERVER*

LAWRENCE OF ARABIA– 1962

Alec Guinness as Prince Feisal in Robert Bolt's Lawrence of Arabia, *a film directed by David Lean. Peter O'Toole played Lawrence.*

GUINNESS, with false nose, pointed beard, flowing robes, cut a majestic figure: wise, proud, sophisticated, witty and wily.

The Wadi Rum, brilliantly photographed by F.A. Young, provided magnificent and unforgettable scenery.

EXIT THE KING – 1963

Alec Guinness as King Berenger the First in Eugène Ionesco's Exit
the King, *directed by George Devine, for the English Stage
Company, Lyceum, Edinburgh. The production transferred to
the Royal Court Theatre.*

Why was I born if not for ever?

BERENGER

'**Y**OU ARE GOING to die in an hour and half,' says the
Queen to the King. 'You are going to die at the end of
the show.' Of all Ionesco's plays, *Exit the King* seems the one
most likely to last.

The Queen describes the 'ceremony of death' as a lot of
fuss about nothing, and quite clearly many in the audience
felt this was true of the play as well. But just when they were
becoming especially restless, Berenger wryly reminded
them it was wonderful even to feel bored if the alternative
was to be dead or dying.

Guinness as the frightened king, hoping against hope
that what he was going through was only a nightmare,
responded magnificently to Ionesco's best writing. There
were two speeches in particular: the first a most moving
prayer to all those who had gone before to teach him how to
resign himself to death; and the second a very amusing
monologue in which he tried desperately to think of *any*
means by which to perpetuate his name after he had gone.

THE FALL OF THE ROMAN EMPIRE – 1964

Alec Guinness as Marcus Aurelius and Christopher Plummer as Commodus in The Fall of the Roman Empire, *a film directed by Anthony Mann.*

EDWARD GIBBON's name was not mentioned. *The Fall of the Roman Empire* was the story of two buddies: the good buddy, played by Stephen Boyd, who should have succeeded to the empire, and the bad buddy, played by Christopher Plummer, who did and destroyed it. The film was a classic confrontation of Beefstake versus High Camp. The high spot was their chariot race and a gladiatorial javelin fight in an improvised arena made with shields.

Guinness played the emperor, a religious philosopher and stoic. He had a long soliloquy on death and was given a magnificent funeral in the snow.

His gently ironic performance ('Please do not bring me his head, I would not know what to do with it') seemed to belong to a more intimate film.

The make-up department had done such a convincing Roman job on his head that it looked as if they had stolen it from some museum.

Alec Guinness is perfect casting for the part, a natural stoic if ever our neurotic age possessed one.
PENELOPE GILLIATT *OBSERVER*

DYLAN – 1964

Louisa Cabot as Thelma Wonderland and Alec Guinness as Dylan Thomas in Sidney Michaels's Dylan, *directed by Peter Glenville at the Plymouth Theatre, New York.*

DYLAN THOMAS, poet, lecturer, drinker, womaniser, refuses to go gently into the good night. Sidney Michaels's episodic play described his disintegration during the last days of a disastrous tour of American universities.

The attraction of the play comes almost entirely from the melancholy tenacity with which Sir Alec Guinness portrays the poet.
HENRY HEWES *SATURDAY REVIEW*

Mr Guinness is an actor who makes you forget that he is acting. One of the most difficult things in the theater is to make convincing a charismatic figure like Dylan Thomas for whom all women seem to be putty and all men willing slaves. Mr Guinness accomplishes this feat with remarkable magnetism within a style of the utmost reserve.
HOWARD TAUBMAN *THE NEW YORK TIMES*

SITUATION HOPELESS – BUT NOT SERIOUS – 1965

Alec Guinness as Herr Frick in Situation Hopeless – But Not Serious, *a film directed by Gottfried Reinhardt.*

GUINNESS played a nice German, a quiet, eccentric, unassuming shop-clerk who hides two American pilots during the Second World War and likes them so much that he doesn't tell them when the war is over.

The film was not seen in England until 1969, and then only briefly.

Though billed as a comedy, Situation Hopeless – But Not Serious *flatly re-establishes that Sir Alec has taken leave of his sense of humour.*

TIME MAGAZINE

DOCTOR ZHIVAGO – 1965

Rita Tushingham as the Girl and Alec Guinness as Yevgraf Zhivago in the film version of Boris Pasternak's Doctor Zhivago, directed by David Lean.

PASTERNAK'S epic love story, set during the Russian Revolution, was a lot of snow and balalaika.

Guinness made an occasional appearance as Zhivago's Bolshevik half-brother, a Red Army general, a member of the secret police. 'I've executed better men than me,' he said.

It was an unrewarding role. Basically he was there to question Zhivago's daughter at the beginning and close of the film, a framing device which could well have been cut.

Potentially the most promising scene, the reunion with his brother, was not improved, for him at any rate, by giving all the dialogue to Omar Sharif and leaving him with the voice-over.

INCIDENT AT VICHY – 1966

Jeremy Kemp as the Major, John Garrie as the Old Jew, Derek Carpenter as the Boy, Brian Blessed as Bayard, Alec Guinness as Von Berg, Dudley Sutton as Lebeau, Anthony Quayle as Leduc, Angus MacKay as Marchand, John Herrington as the Captain, Andrew Ray as the Waiter, Nigel Davenport as Monceau, Jack Howlett as the 1st Detective, Darryl Kavann as the 2nd Detective, Derek Smith as the Professor and (seated on the floor) David Calderisi in Arthur Miller's Incident at Vichy, *directed by Peter Wood at the Phoenix Theatre.*

It's not your guilt I want, it's your responsibility.

THE INCIDENT at Vichy is the summary rounding-up of Jews in 1942 and their despatch to the concentration camps and furnaces.

Arthur Miller's most striking premise was that the Nazis were only doing what the rest of the world wanted them to do. Given the subject matter, it was difficult for an audience not to be involved, but his long one-acter, played without interval, remained a debate on the Holocaust rather than a play.

Guinness was cast as the only gentile, a dilettante Austrian prince, who has been detained by mistake. A cultured man, with a deep love of music, he takes no interest in politics. What disgusts him most about the Nazis is their unspeakable *vulgarity*.

Finally, forced to acknowledge his complicity, the prince gives his life that a Jew might live in an act of self-sacrifice Sydney Carton might have envied.

Sitting there for much of the time just listening, Guinness's role was to record the prince's distress and mounting horror.

Sir Alec, with his surgical delicacy, exposes the prince's mind, showing how the man has grown since he entered the place of detention as a man incredulous, inquiring, yet apart: no actor can study a silence as Guinness can.

J.C. TREWIN *ILLUSTRATED LONDON NEWS*

MACBETH – 1966

Alec Guinness as Macbeth and Simone Signoret as Lady Macbeth in Shakespeare's Macbeth, *directed by William Gaskill, for the English Stage Company, at the Royal Court Theatre.*

THE PRODUCTION, on a bare box-stage, brilliantly lit throughout, was so uncompromisingly Brechtian that most critics were totally alienated.

Guinness's performance was not helped by the great film actress's French-American accent and her unfamiliarity with Shakespeare's language and rhythms.

The notices were so bad that William Gaskill threatened to ban the critics from all future productions at the Royal Court. There was a blazing row in the Press and calls for Gaskill's sacking. Finally, he was forced to retract.

It must have taken a great deal of work to persuade Alec Guinness to give a performance so totally colourless as his Macbeth.
B.A. YOUNG *FINANCIAL TIMES*

It is a brilliant reading, brilliantly sustained, but at every point it cries out for just the pompous wardrobe and mobs of stage-listeners Gaskill has banished.
RONALD BRYDEN *OBSERVER*

It says much for Sir Alec's gift of anonymity that although he is standing and speaking in full view of the audience, with only the witches and Banquo present, it is two or three minutes before we even notice him. If ever The Invisible Man *is dramatised, Sir Alec will be ideal casting; but Macbeth is not his part. This urbane Scot could never unseam anyone 'from the nave to the chaps'.*
HUGH LEONARD *PLAYS AND PLAYERS*

HOTEL PARADISO – 1966

Gina Lollobrigida as Marcelle Cot, Alec Guinness as Benedict Boniface and Robert Morley as Henri Cot in the film version of Georges Feydeau and Maurice Desvallière's Hotel Paradiso, *directed by Peter Glenville.*

HOTEL PARADISO was not released in England until five years later, by which time the Feydeau bubbly had gone decidedly flat.

The actors threw themselves into their parts with a great deal of stagey energy, which revealed all the mechanics of farce without providing many of the laughs.

Guinness, very stylish, was really too dapper for the hen-pecked husband; while Gina Lollobrigida looked more like a *cocotte* than the epitome of bourgeois respectability she was meant to be playing.

Peter Glenville, who had directed the original stage production, opened the play out to embrace *La Belle Époque* and himself. He appeared as Feydeau, who observes all that is going on and then puts it into a play – a silly and totally unnecessary conceit.

THE QUILLER MEMORANDUM –
1966

George Segal as Quiller and Alec Guinness as Pol in The Quiller Memorandum, *a film directed by Michael Anderson.*

THE QUILLER MEMORANDUM was a dull spy thriller: a story of neo-Nazis in contemporary Germany, and the blue-eyed agent who sets out to find their Berlin headquarters.

Guinness played the agent's control. His opening scene, set in the 1936 Olympic Stadium, drily scripted and wittily acted, raised expectations which the rest of the film failed to deliver.

Guinness had but four short scenes, spread throughout the film, each shorter than the last. He brought to the role a camp voice, a common little moustache, cold shifting eyes and a jaunty insensitivity which was very funny in an unnerving sort of way.

When the film was shown in Germany all references to neo-Nazism were deleted.

Gordon Jackson as Mr Booker and Alec Guinness as 'Mrs Artminster' in Wise Child

WISE CHILD – 1967

Alec Guinness as 'Mrs Artminster' in Simon Gray's Wise Child, directed by John Dexter at Wyndham's Theatre.

SIMON GRAY's first West End play, a murderous black comedy, in the Joe Orton manner, was set in a seedy boarding-house, run by a homosexual hotelier with a religious bent.

The leading character was a criminal-on-the-run who had been forced to disguise himself as a mother with a grown-up son by a kinky lad with a mother-complex.

The dialogue was often very funny. The play was less satisfactory. What worked best was Guinness's female impersonation, and his voice alternating, often in mid-sentence, between gruff thug and genteel Tunbridge Wells. It was a bit like watching Magwitch in drag.

THE COCKTAIL PARTY – 1968

Pauline Jameson as Lavinia Chamberlayne, Alec Guinness as Sir Henry Harcourt-Reilly, and Michael Aldridge as Edward Chamberlayne in T.S. Eliot's The Cocktail Party, *directed by Alec Guinness at the Chichester Festival Theatre. The production transferred to Wyndham's Theatre, and then to the Theatre Royal, Haymarket, in 1969.*

E LIOT's uneasy mixture of tiresome social chatter and religious allegory turned out to be much easier than everybody had thought eighteen years previously at its premiere at the Edinburgh Festival.

Guinness once again played the Unidentified Guest, half-God, half-psychiatrist, who sends a woman to a horrible martyrdom in the jungle. He looked like a very satanic Sigmund Freud. (He shaved off the beard when the play came into London.)

His production, notable for its reverence and clarity, had the cold artificiality the text demands. The second act in particular, beautifully acted and spoken by him and Eileen Atkins, was very powerful indeed in its ominous stillness.

Guinness effaces himself almost totally. No other actor so firmly rejects any temptation to showiness. Yet in this poetic and mystical territory his command and authority are absolute.
PETER LEWIS *DAILY MAIL*

His greatest achievement, however, is that he creates a texture of lightness, almost of gaiety which deflates any latent pomposity.
FRANK MARCUS *SUNDAY TELEGRAPH*

THE COMEDIANS – 1968

Peter Ustinov as Ambassador Pineda, Alec Guinness as Major Jones (in disguise as a black cook) and Richard Burton as Mr Brown in Graham Greene's The Comedians, *a film directed by Peter Glenville.*

Greene's *The Comedians* (the word is used in the French sense, meaning actors) was set in Papa Doc's corrupt and brutal Haiti. The political melodrama was always more interesting than the love affair of the leading characters, played by Elizabeth Taylor and Richard Burton.

Guinness was cast as the braggart Jones, a fake-major, crook and gun-runner. The man's shiftiness and bogusness had an almost comic innocence. The final confession ('I'm an awful liar, old man') was easily the most moving scene in the film. It turned out that he had spent the war running ENSA concert parties.

Opposite: Alec Guinness in The Old Country *1977*

1970s

TWELFTH NIGHT – 1970

Alec Guinness as Malvolio and Joan Plowright as Viola in Shakespeare's Twelfth Night, *directed by John Dexter for ATV.*

Nobody had worked out how to present Shakespeare on television. Illyria was a very dull, cardboardy place.

Guinness was amusingly smug when Malvolio was dreaming of making love to his mistress and lording it over her kinsmen. If he didn't exactly dance for joy, he certainly trod more lightly and waved a yellow-stockinged, cross-garter'd leg in what he mistakenly thought was a sexy manner.

On his final exit, having been most notoriously abused for his presumption, Malvolio threw down his chain of office and threatened to be revenged on the pack of them. It was a threat it would have been possible to take quite seriously, had not the director opted for comic-pathos of the glibbest kind and cut from the actor's face to the stockings which were now round his ankles.

TIME OUT OF MIND – 1970

Alec Guinness as John and Mark Kingston as Bob Tyndall in Bridget Boland's Time Out of Mind, *directed by Stephen Barry at the Yvonne Arnaud Theatre, Guildford.*

Time out of mind was about an elderly laboratory assistant in a government research establishment who had accidentally discovered the elixir of life in 1366.

The play did not come into London.

CROMWELL – 1970

Alec Guinness as Charles I in Cromwell, *a film written and directed by Ken Hughes. Richard Harris played Cromwell.*

Cromwell was a popular mixture of over-simplified history, spectacle, two battles (Edgehill and Naseby), and the trial and execution of a king on a charge of high treason.

The script contained many familiar lines, yet far from giving the dialogue a greater authenticity they served only to make the actors appear even more artificial and stagey.

Guinness's Charles I, played with a slight Scottish accent and a slight speech impediment, was a portrait of passive grandeur and cavalier melancholy. He might have sat for Van Dyck. He was *tristesse* personified, a proud, aloof, intractable man, presuming on the Divine Right of Kings. 'I am no ordinary person, sir.'

There were some telling close-ups of his face during the trial at Westminster, revealing anger, unease, and also bemusement that he should be held responsible for all the rape and pillage committed during the Civil War.

It was a pity that he was denied two attested theatrical moments: firstly the dropping of his gold-topped cane and nobody bending to retrieve it; and secondly, though he was given the line ('The morning air will do me good') there was, sadly, no long walk through the park to the scaffold.

SCROOGE – 1970

Alec Guinness as Marley's Ghost in Leslie Bricusse's Scrooge, *a film directed by Ronald Neame. Albert Finney played Scrooge.*

Leslie bricusse's musical tried to do for *A Christmas Carol* what Lionel Bart's *Oliver!* had already done for *Oliver Twist*, and he failed.

Scrooge was a lot of humbug: skinflint Ebenezer was so transformed in character by the end that he dressed up as Father Christmas, a sentimentality even Charles Dickens baulked at. The musical numbers, with the possible exception of the very Bartish *Thank You Very Much* added nothing whatever; and even this needed some proper choreography.

Guinness, bandaged, manacled, and all in grey, was a surprisingly camp Old Marley, undulating his way through hell, carrying his chains like so many handbags. It was one of his least appealing performances. Patrick Gibbs, writing in the *Daily Telegraph*, thought he looked like Old Mother Riley dipped in flour.

A VOYAGE ROUND MY FATHER –
1971

Alec Guinness as Father and Jeremy Brett as Son in John Mortimer's A Voyage Round My Father, *directed by Ronald Eyre at the Theatre Royal, Haymarket.*

A VOYAGE ROUND MY FATHER acted like some isolated pages from a forthcoming biography.

Guinness was cast as John Mortimer's barrister father who in middle age suddenly went blind, refused to take any notice of his disability, and carried on as if it did not exist. It was a role which had been created by Mark Dignam at Greenwich Theatre and which would later be played by Laurence Olivier on television.

The play's most arresting moment came when somebody dared to ask why everybody was pretending the father was not blind when he so obviously was.

Sir Alec's performance is so complete in its grasp of how such a man would move, look, speak and behave to his companions that for me it is beyond praise.
B.A. YOUNG *FINANCIAL TIMES*

His sense of comedy, his delicacy, his meticulous attention to physical detail, and his suggestion of depth are masterfully integrated; it is his best performance in recent years. His sad clown's face is like a landscape, registering every nuance of changing light.
FRANK MARCUS *SUNDAY TELEGRAPH*

Opposite: *Alec Guinness as Father in* A Voyage Round My Father.

HITLER – THE LAST TEN DAYS –
1973

Alec Guinness as Adolf Hitler in Hitler – The Last Ten Days, *a film directed by Ennio de Concinci.*

HITLER – THE LAST TEN DAYS was a dramatic reconstruction of the last days in the Berlin bunker, based on the memoirs of Gerhard Boldt. The film relied on the events themselves, rather than any cinematic flair, to hold an audience's attention. The director, using interspersed newsreel footage to a waltz-time accompaniment, favoured an ironic approach to his material.

The most memorable moments were the funny ones: Hitler's birthday, for instance, and his marriage to Eva Braun ('Are you of Aryan descent? Are you suffering from any hereditary diseases?' asked an understandably nervous registrar). There was also his farewell gift to his staff (two cyanide capsules and a portrait of himself), and, most hilarious of all, the scene where everybody was telling everybody else how they were going to commit suicide.

On learning of the Fuehrer's death, the whole bunker celebrated by lighting up cigarettes – the cigarettes he had banned while he was still alive. If this were fact, it certainly seemed like fiction. So much of the film played like some ludicrous black farce that it was not surprising if audiences were unable to take the movie seriously.

Hitler's paranoia (*I cannot be wrong!! Everything I say and do is history!!*) had undeniable power, but many people, including Guinness himself, felt that big hysterical screaming was not his forte as an actor.

But capable performance as it is, he remains stubbornly himself, a fine actor acting.
DEREK MALCOLM *GUARDIAN*

Beautiful actor though he is, I don't think Sir Alec can submerge his own nature sufficiently to give us the gang-boss, the vengeful torturer.
DILYS POWELL *SUNDAY TIMES*

FRATELLO SOLE, SORELLA LUNA
– 1972

Graham Faulkner as Francis and Alec Guinness as Pope Innocent III in Fratello Sole, Sorella Luna, *a film directed by Franco Zeffirelli. English title:* Brother Sun, Sister Moon.

THE FILM was an account of the early life of St Francis of Assisi, who, no doubt, for good box-office reasons, was equated with modern hippies, drop-outs and Jesus-freaks.

Guinness appeared right at the end, sumptuously robed in the most sumptuous of settings. The Pope is so deeply moved when Francis quotes the lines from Matthew about laying your treasure not on earth but in heaven that he kneels down and kisses his feet.

HABEAS CORPUS – 1973

Patricia Hayes as Mrs Swabb, Margaret Courtenay as Muriel Wicksteed, Phyllida Law as Constance Wicksteed, Roddy Maude-Roxby as Canon Throbbing, Madeline Smith as Felicity Rumpers, Joan Sanderson as Lady Rumpers, Christopher Good as Dennis Wicksteed and Alec Guinness as Arthur Wicksteed in Alan Bennett's Habeas Corpus, *directed by Ronald Eyre at the Lyric Theatre.*

HABEAS CORPUS – 1973

Sex isn't something that happens over-night, you know.

Habeas corpus was a story of medical misconduct. The stage, to all intents and purposes, was bare. A Magritte-looking sky served as a back-cloth. Props were kept to the minimum. The odd telephone was hurled into the wings. The dialogue, spoken for the most part directly to the audience, was a happy mixture of Donald McGill picture-postcard vulgarity and literary pastiche. The word 'farce' was never used. The real subject matter of Alan Bennett's play was not the sexual fantasies and frustrations of the characters (all comic stereotypes) but death.

Guinness was cast as a sly and lecherous GP. His little dance at the end of the play was almost invariably misunderstood by the audience who, presumably, would not have received it with such obvious delight had they realised the top-hat-tails-and-cane routine, which kept starting and stopping, was a series of heart-attacks.

He is masterly in his ability to put poison into a deadpan line.
B.A. YOUNG *FINANCIAL TIMES*

Alec Guinness in Habeas Corpus.

A FAMILY AND A FORTUNE – 1975

Rachel Kempson as Blanche Gaveston, Margaret Leighton as Matty Seaton, Graham Swannell as Mark Gaveston, Bruce Bould as Clement Gaveston, Anthony Nicholls as Edgar Gaveston, Alec Guinness as Dudley Gaveston, Nicola Pagett as Justine Gaveston and Donald Eccles as Oliver Seaton in Julian Mitchell's adaptation from Ivy Compton-Burnett's A Family and a Fortune, directed by Alan Strachan at the Apollo Theatre.

IVY COMPTON-BURNETT's novels are built almost entirely on dialogue, but that does not mean they necessarily make good theatre.

Guinness, as the second son of an impoverished upper-middle-class Edwardian family who unexpectedly come into a fortune, caught perfectly the man's fastidious meekness and his enormous self-respect. The production, however, was quite dead, the highly stylised conversation, despite its undeniable wit, malice, and irony, cutting no dramatic ice.

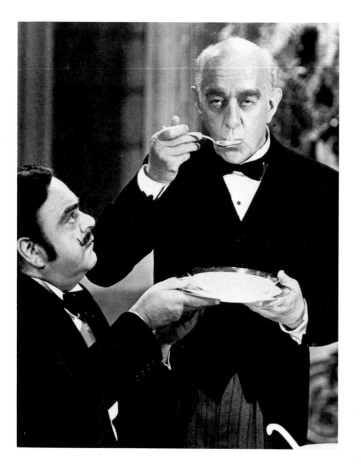

MURDER BY DEATH – 1976

James Coco as Milo Perier and Alec Guinness as Bensonmum in Neil Simon's Murder by Death, a film directed by Robert Moore.

A<small>N ECCENTRIC MILLIONAIRE</small> invites five famous fictional detectives to dinner and a murder. The detectives are Sam Spade, Charlie Chan, Hercule Poirot, Miss Marples and *The Thin Man* husband-and-wife team

Neil Simon's send-up of the classic 1930s/1940s detective movie was very much an in-joke for film buffs and lovers of theatrical high camp.

Guinness, rolling his eyeballs back under his eyes, played the blind butler who serves soup from an empty tureen and lights fires in the middle of beds (under the impression that the bed is a grate). The scenes he shared with Nancy Walker, as a deaf-and-dumb foreign maid who can't read English, were hilarious.

YAHOO – 1976

Alec Guinness as Jonathan Swift in Yahoo, directed by Alan Strachan at the Queen's Theatre.

Y<small>AHOO</small> was an anthology of verse, prose, pamphlets and letters by Jonathan Swift. It was a civilised, literate evening's entertainment, notable for its stylish elegance rather than its savagery, and should, perhaps, in the circumstances, have been called *Houyhnhnm.*

Guinness's dry, mild tones were admirably suited to the bitter irony of Swift's solution to the Irish famine as expressed in *A Modest Proposal*:

I have been assured by a very knowing American of my acquaintance in London that a young healthy child well nursed is at a year old a most delicious, nourishing, and wholesome food, whether stewed, roasted, baked, or boiled, and I make no doubt it will equally serve in a fricasise, or a ragoust.

His manner is unswervingly serene and his very larynx sounds as if he's been gargling with honey; it is the music, not the content, of the lines that seems perpetually to absorb him.
BENEDICT NIGHTINGALE *NEW STATESMAN*

Yahoo does not provide an evening of delight, nor yet of hope. But to see Alec Guinness, the leading houyhnhnm of our stage, engage all his formidable powers of piercing intelligence and revealing insights with the torn heart and bleeding mind of Jonathan Swift provided something even rarer in the theatre: true satisfaction.
BERNARD LEVIN *SUNDAY TIMES*

THE OLD COUNTRY – 1977

Alec Guinness as Hilary and Rachel Kempson as Bron in Alan Bennett's The Old Country, directed by Clifford Williams at the Queen's Theatre.

The best disguise of all is to be exactly what you say you are. Nobody ever believes that.

HILARY

THE PLAY is set in Russia, though the audience does not know this until the end of the first act.

Hilary, a spy who defected fourteen years previously, is invited home. He rejects the invitation. He sees no point in going back to the old country when the England he knew and loved no longer exists. 'How can I come home? I am home. I am a Soviet citizen.' But he has no choice. He has to go back. He is part of an exchange for a Russian spy.

Hilary constantly uses irony as a camouflage for the guilt and despair he feels but never expresses. The tragedy of his life could always be seen clearly in Guinness's face; and the irony was, perhaps, even more lethal for being understated.

Alec Guinness gives one of his finest performances in the role: both erect and crumbling, he conveys a sense of tenacious indecision and dignified self-disgust.

JOHN PETER *SUNDAY TIMES*

STAR WARS – 1977

Alec Guinness as Ben (Obi-Wan) Kenobi in Star Wars, *a film directed by George Lucas.*

A LONG TIME AGO and far away in another galaxy. . . . *Star Wars*, commercially one of the most successful films ever made, was a mixture of science-fiction, fairy tale, western, comic-strip and gangster movie.

The actors inevitably played a very supporting role to the stunning visual effects. Guinness was cast as the last of the Jedi knights, guardian of peace and justice, a good man with extraordinary sensory powers, who dies by the laser-beam sword at the hands of the Forces of Evil, represented by a splendid Teutonic figure in a black-helmeted mask.

Guinness, in his cowl and white beard, looking like a wise old monk, had no difficulty whatsoever in conveying the man's goodness, idealism and inner strength. He was nominated for an 'Oscar' as the best supporting actor, and appeared briefly in two sequels, *The Empire Strikes Back* and *Return of the Jedi*.

It was a rather simple outline of a good man. I tried to make him uncomplicated. I'm cunning enough now to know that to be simple carries a lot of weight.
ALEC GUINNESS QUOTED BY TIME MAGAZINE

Depend on this actor to make obscure twaddle sound like lucid philosophy.
FELIX BARKER *EVENING NEWS*

CAESAR AND CLEOPATRA – 1977

Alec Guinness as Julius Caesar in George Bernard Shaw's Caesar and Cleopatra, *directed by James Cellan Jones for Southern Television. Genevieve Bujold played Cleopatra.*

G UINNESS'S foxy, paternalistic emperor was a perfect marriage of outward gentleness allied to inner steely strength. The wit ('Always take a throne when it is offered you') was very dry.

The production's most dramatic moment came when Caesar learned of Cleopatra's murder of a political opponent and coldly upbraided her for her folly. His repulsion and scorn were such that it seemed as if his celebrated clemency might end there and then.

TINKER, TAILOR, SOLDIER, SPY –
1979

Alec Guinness as George Smiley in John Le Carré's Tinker,
Tailor, Soldier, Spy, *directed by John Irvin for BBC Television.*

GEORGE SMILEY, luckless, inconsolable and utterly lonely, is brought out of retirement to flush out the Augean
stables. His task is to find the mole who has infiltrated the
top five in the Circus he ran before he was sacked.

The convoluted and dense narrative, spread over seven
fifty-minute episodes, certainly took its time, leaving the
nation deeply baffled as to what was going on in British
Intelligence.

Guinness held the series together by his own personal
authority, no less formidable for being so much of the time
passive. He said little. He listened a great deal. ('So hard to
be a geriatric ear', he confided to John Le Carré.) His

intelligence was transparent, his horn-rimmed spectacles
alone suggesting a wealth of knowledge and experience.

Pursing his lips, looking thoughtful and purposeful, he
had the heavy quiet that commands. His final summing-up
was brutally to the point: 'There will have to be some
re-deployment (long pause) for those of you who wish to
remain in the service.'

Smiley was one of Guinness's most subtle performances.

*It is enough, however, just to gaze in wonder at the art of Alec
Guinness. All gentle nuances and understatement. Magnificat.*
MARTIN JACKSON *DAILY MAIL*

*Alec Guinness is undoubtedly one of Britain's – which is to say, the
world's – great actors, but he is an even greater non-actor. It is what
he does not do that makes him so compelling.*
ROSALIE HORNER *DAILY EXPRESS*

Opposite: *Alec Guinness in* Little Dorrit *1987*

1980s

LITTLE LORD FAUNTLEROY – 1980

Ricky Shroder as Ceddie Errol and Alec Guinness as the Earl of Dorincourt in the television version of Frances Eliza Hodgson Burnett's Little Lord Fauntleroy, *directed by Jack Gold.*

THIS CHARMING and witty version of the famous children's classic was made for American television but shown in cinemas abroad. It deserves to be better known. The film is genuinely moving.

Guinness played the mean, gouty, old earl who is shamed into turning the slums on his estate into a model village by an amiable and outspoken American urchin whose spunky decency melts every heart.

Ricky Shroder's precocity in the title role was very appealing. It was a performance without curls, the producers having wisely decided to cut them, along with the velvet suit and Van Dyck collar which made only one nominal and reluctant appearance. 'It goes with the job,' said Ceddie.

The relationship between the boy and the lonely old man ('I'm not well-liked, but he finds me likeable') was beautifully judged: sentimental without being mawkish.

RAISE THE TITANIC – 1980

Alec Guinness as John Bigalow and Richard Jordan as Dirk Pitt in a film version of Clive Cussler's Raise the Titanic, *directed by Jerry Jameson.*

T HE STORY described the salvaging of the great luxury liner from its icy Atlantic grave for the sake of the radio-active minerals concealed on board.

The film proved a financial disaster of Titanic proportions. It was reported that the model of the ship alone cost £3 million pounds – £500,000 more than the original.

Guinness had the small role of one of the survivors, a former cargo officer, now living in a quaint Cornish village and reminiscing over large pink gins.

SMILEY'S PEOPLE – 1982

Alec Guinness as George Smiley, on location, for John Le Carré's Smiley's People, *directed by Simon Langton for BBC Television.*

I T WAS GENERALLY agreed that *Smiley's People*, a complicated story, full of contrasts and full of gaps, was less complicated than *Tinker, Tailor, Soldier, Spy*; though for audiences lost for a second time in Le Carré's labyrinth of international espionage, this was little comfort.

Smiley was an old spy in a hurry, dragged out of retirement once more to pursue his own private war against his great Russian rival, who appeared only in the last few minutes of the last episode.

There were numerous close-ups of Guinness's face just listening; the only thing the face ever gave away was formidable intellect and authority.

It was Smiley's non-reaction to answers, questions, statements, even greetings, which was the most striking aspect of Guinness's performance. Hailed by former colleagues and members of staff with a mixture of awe and affection, he invariably kept his distance. 'You do remember me, don't you?' pleaded one poor individual. 'Of course,' he replied in a voice which gave no reassurance that he did. You could hear the portcullis coming down. It was chilling.

I try to keep it real and simple and remember that it's the other that actors who come in and supply the colour. ALEC GUINNESS QUOTED BY MICHAEL BILLINGTON *THE NEW YORK TIMES*

Sir Alec Guinness's performance, condemned by some for its passivity, strikes me as great film acting pared down to the dry bone. Only an actor who has done it all can now do so little and get away with it. HERBERT KRETZMER *DAILY MAIL*

LOVESICK – 1983

Dudley Moore as Saul Benjamin and Alec Guinness as Sigmund Freud in Lovesick, *a film written and directed by Marshall Brickman.*

L OVESICK, a thin comedy about a New York psychoanalyst who falls in love with one of his patients, was acted by Dudley Moore with unexpected seriousness.

Guinness was cast as his fantasy Freud who drops in from time to time to offer advice, insights and commentary. It wasn't much of a part, the wit not rising much above the level of Freud never having heard of a Freudian slip.

EDWIN – 1984

Alec Guinness as Sir Fennimore Truscott and Renee Asherson as Lady Truscott in John Mortimer's Edwin, *directed by Rodney Bennett for Anglia Television.*

Sir Fennimore Truscott is a retired High Court judge who conducts his private life as though he is still sitting in court dispensing justice. He suspects his wife of having had an affair with the next-door neighbour and puts them through a mock trial for possible infidelity. He charges the neighbour of 'rogering' his wife and fathering his child, the unseen Edwin. When the two men actually meet Edwin, after many years' absence, he turns out to be such a prig, that neither of them wants to be his father.

The judge, for all his judicial wit and irony, is totally without humour. Guinness turned the old man's obsession, pomposity and prickliness into something both touching and amusing.

THE MERCHANT OF VENICE – 1984

Alec Guinness as Shylock in Shakespeare's The Merchant of Venice, *directed by Patrick Garland at the Chichester Festival Theatre.*

Guinness's elderly Levantine was a sophisticated, well-bred figure of blinkered obduracy. The loss of his wife's ring (*I would not have given it for a wilderness of monkeys*) meant far more to him than the elopement of his daughter with a Christian.

There was an unforgettable moment during the trial when, having come to collect his pound of flesh, Shylock bent to place his ear next to Antonio's chest so that he could hear the beat of the heart he intended to stop.

But, for the most part, the performance was in such a low key, the acting so minimal, that for those members of the audience not actually sitting in the rows immediately next to Chichester's open stage, it often seemed as if he were doing nothing.

Guinness does what only a really good actor has the courage to do. He resists all temptations to impress.
FELIX BARKER *PLAYS AND PLAYERS*

Shylock is a small role, but in most performances his presence spreads throughout the play: not here, for when Guinness is not on the stage it is quite easy to forget Shylock is in the play at all.
MICHAEL RATCLIFFE *OBSERVER*

Guinness has been away from the stage for seven years. He must be wondering why he came back.
ROBERT HEWISON *SUNDAY TIMES*

A PASSAGE TO INDIA – 1984

Alec Guinness as Professor Godbole in the film version of E.M. Forster's A Passage to India, *directed by David Lean.*

IT SEEMED INCREDIBLE when all the other Indian characters were played by Indian actors that David Lean should cast Guinness as a Brahmin mystic.

Godbole, who represents the old Hindu tradition of love, is, perhaps, along with Mrs Moore, the most difficult character in the novel to translate to the screen. Guinness's few appearances (so few they might as well have been cut) were pretty meaningless.

MONSIGNOR QUIXOTE – 1985

Leo McKern as Sancho and Alec Guinness as Father Quixote in Graham Greene's Monsignor Quixote, *directed by Rodney Bennett for Thames Television.*

GRAHAM GREENE's picaresque novella is about a humble parish priest who, unexpectedly and much against his will, is promoted to Monsignor. He and Sancho (the Communist ex-mayor) spend much of their time discussing Theology and Marxism.

Guinness's performance caught unerringly 'the muffled voice of uncertainty': the despair and doubts of a man who desperately wants to believe in God. 'I *think* I touch Him,' he said. His vulnerability was most moving.

The scene which lingers longest in the memory is the one in which the priest says Mass at an imaginary communion. Such was the actor's total involvement, such was its power, that in an extraordinary way it felt as if Quixote was no longer there and that Guinness himself was saying the Mass.

I am not sure that Guinness, though he was Greene's own choice, was quite the man to play this holy fool. That voice with the curves and polish of a cello. Those really terrifying eyes. Sometimes nothing moves in his face but his eyes and they do so with the heart-stopping click of a cocking-revolver.

NANCY BANKS-SMITH *GUARDIAN*

LITTLE DORRIT – 1987

Alec Guinness as William Dorrit in the film version of Charles Dickens's Little Dorrit, *directed by Christine Edzard.*

THE GREAT strength of Christine Edzard's film lay in the excellence of the cast, Guinness's definitive performance as the 'Father of Marshalsea' being just one of many definitive performances.

The forlorn gentility, the maudlin self-pity (*I have endured everything*), the selfishness, vanity, foolishness, complacency, hypocrisy (*I couldn't think of sacrificing you – my conscience would not allow it*) were all quite perfect.

The shabby levées in the debtors' prison where Dorrit accepts gifts of money as if they are tributes to some minor royalty were beautifully acted; while the final scene, at the banquet to celebrate his eldest daughter's wedding, when he rises to his feet to make a speech, and, after an interminable pause, welcomes the guests to the Marshalsea, was unforgettable in its pathos.

Alec Guinness's William Dorrit, a haughty seedy gentleman-sponger, must be ranked among the six best performances he's ever given.
ALEXANDER WALKER *EVENING STANDARD*

A HANDFUL OF DUST – 1988

Alec Guinness as Mr Todd in the film version of Evelyn Waugh's
A Handful of Dust, *directed by Charles Sturridge.*

THE NOVEL, which had its origins in the breakdown of Waugh's own marriage, is a brittle satire on the self-indulgent upper classes between the wars.

There is nothing in the film to prepare an audience for the truly shattering climax, in which the hero finds himself held against his will, in the South American jungle, forced to read the works of Charles Dickens over and over again to a crazy, illiterate half-caste.

The final section needed an actor of Guinness's weight. The very slight emphasis he gave to Todd's deceptively simple statement, 'Yes, you *shall* read to me,' was enough to send a shiver down the spine.

A WALK IN THE WOODS – 1988

Edward Herrmann as John Honeyman and Alec Guinness as Andrey Lvovich Botvinnik in Lee Blessing's A Walk in the Woods, directed by Ronald Eyre at the Comedy Theatre.

A SOVIET diplomat and an American negotiator meet privately in a wood near Geneva to see if they can come to any agreement away from the conference table.

A Walk in the Woods, a facile conversation piece on nuclear arms control, comes to the conclusion that since neither of the great powers is serious about reducing arms, the destruction of the world is inevitable, and the time up till then will be filled with interminable discussions, always ending in deadlock. The last moments of the play blatantly echo Estragon and Vladimir waiting for Godot.

Guinness played the weary diplomat with a reputation for saying 'no' longer than anybody else. He was at his wittiest, driest, most relaxed, most disarming, and never more in earnest than when he was being most frivolous. His was the more sympathetic role, Soviet friendliness and irony being infinitely preferable to American rigidity and priggishness.

Awards and Honours

1950   National Board of Review Award
        Best Actor: *Kind Hearts and Coronets*

1950   Picturegoer Gold Medal
        Most Popular Actor

1952   Academy of Motion Pictures Arts and Sciences Award
        Nomination for Best Actor: *The Lavender Hill Mob*

1955   CBE

1956   Office Catholique Internationale du Cinema
        Award presented to the star of *The Prisoner*

1957   Academy of Motion Picture Arts and Sciences Award
        'Oscar'. Best Actor: *The Bridge on the River Kwai*
        New York Film Critics' Circle Award
        Best Actor: *The Bridge on the River Kwai*
        National Board of Review Award
        Best Actor: *The Bridge on the River Kwai*
        British Film Academy Award
        Best Actor: *The Bridge on the River Kwai*
        Golden Globe Award
        Best Actor: *The Bridge on the River Kwai*

1958   Academy of Motion Pictures Arts and Sciences Award
        Best screenplay based on material from another medium:
        The Horse's Mouth

1959   Knighthood

1960   Evening Standard Drama Award
        Best Actor: *Ross*

1962   Hon. D.Fine Arts, Boston College

1962   Berlin Film Festival
        David O. Selznick Gold Laurel Award for adding to
        international understanding

1963   Plays and Players Award *
        Best Performance: *Exit the King*

1964   Antoinette Perry Award
        'Tony'. Best Actor: *Dylan*

1977   Hon. D.Litt. (Oxon.)

1977   Academy of Motion Pictures Arts and Sciences
        Nomination for Best Supporting Actor: *Star Wars*

1977   Variety Club of Great Britain Award
        Best Actor: *The Old Country*

1978   Academy of Motion Pictures Arts and Sciences Award
        Honorary 'Oscar' for advancing the art of screen acting
        through a host of memorable and distinguished
        performances

1980   British Academy of Film and Television Arts Award
        Best Actor: *Tinker, Tailor, Soldier, Spy*

1982   British Academy of Film and Television Arts Award
        Best Actor: *Smiley's People*

1985   *Blessings in Disguise* published

1985   Shakespeare Prize for services to English literature

1987   Film Society of Lincoln Center
        The society paid homage to the actor for 40 years of
        unforgettable contribution to the movies

1988   Berlin Film Festival Golden Bear Award
        Special 'Oscar' for services to the cinema

1989   The Society of West End Theatre Special Award

* *Plays and Players Award is awarded on the voting of the London
  theatre critics.*

THEATRE

DATE	TITLE	PLAYWRIGHT	ROLE	DIRECTOR	THEATRE
1934					
Apr	Libel!	Edward Wooll	Junior Counsel	Leon M. Lion	Playhouse
Aug	Queer Cargo	Noel Langley	Chinese Coolie French Pirate English Sailor	Reginald Bach	Piccadilly
Nov	Hamlet	William Shakespeare	Third Player Osric	John Gielgud	New
1935					
Jul	Noah	André Obey translated by Arthur Wilmurt	The Wolf	Michel Saint-Denis	New
Oct	Romeo and Juliet	William Shakespeare	Sampson Apothecary	John Gielgud	New
1936					
May	The Seagull	Anton Chekhov translated by Theodore Komisarjevsky	Workman (later) Yakov	Theodore Komisarjevsky	New

1936/1937 The Old Vic Company at the Old Vic Theatre

DATE	TITLE	PLAYWRIGHT	ROLE	DIRECTOR	THEATRE
1936					
Sept	Love's Labour's Lost	William Shakespeare	Boyet	Tyrone Guthrie	
Nov	As You Like It	William Shakespeare	Le Beau William	Esmé Church	
	The Witch of Edmonton	Thomas Dekker†	Old Thorney	Michel Saint-Denis	
1937					
Jan	Hamlet	William Shakespeare	Reynaldo Osric	Tyrone Guthrie	
Feb	Twelfth Night	William Shakespeare	Sir Andrew Aguecheek	Tyrone Guthrie	
Apr	Henry V	William Shakespeare	Duke of Exeter	Tyrone Guthrie	
Jun	Hamlet	William Shakespeare	Reynaldo Player Queen Osric	Tyrone Guthrie	Kronborg Castle, Elsinore

1937/1938 John Gielgud Season at the Queen's Theatre

DATE	TITLE	PLAYWRIGHT	ROLE	DIRECTOR	THEATRE
1937					
Sep	Richard II	William Shakespeare	Aumerle Groom	John Gielgud	
Nov	The School for Scandal	Richard Brinsley Sheridan	Snake	Tyrone Guthrie	
1938					
Jan	Three Sisters	Anton Chekhov translated by Constance Garnett	Fedotik	Michel Saint-Denis	
Apr	The Merchant of Venice	William Shakespeare	Lorenzo	John Gielgud	
Jun	The Doctor's Dilemma	George Bernard Shaw	Louis Dubedat	Bernard Miles	Richmond, Surrey

1938 The Old Vic Company at The Old Vic Theatre

DATE	TITLE	PLAYWRIGHT	ROLE	DIRECTOR	THEATRE
Sep	Trelawny of the 'Wells'	Arthur Wing Pinero	Arthur Gower	Tyrone Guthrie	
Oct	Hamlet	William Shakespeare	Hamlet	Tyrone Guthrie	
Dec	The Rivals	Richard Brinsley Sheridan	Bob Acres	Esmé Church	

1939 The Old Vic Company Tour of Egypt and Europe

DATE	TITLE	PLAYWRIGHT	ROLE	DIRECTOR	THEATRE
Jan/Apr					
	Hamlet	William Shakespeare	Hamlet	Tyrone Guthrie	
	Henry V	William Shakespeare	Chorus	Tyrone Guthrie	
	The Rivals	Richard Brinsley Sheridan	Bob Acres	Esmé Church	
	Libel!	Edward Wooll	Emile Flordon	Leon M. Lion	
Jun	The Ascent of F.6	W.H. Auden and Christopher Isherwood	Michael Ransom	Rupert Doone	Old Vic
Jul	Romeo and Juliet	William Shakespeare	Romeo	Willard Stoker	Perth
Dec	Great Expectations	Charles Dickens adapted by Alec Guinness	Herbert Pocket	George Devine	Rudolph Steiner Hall
1940					
Mar	Cousin Muriel	Clemence Dane	Richard Meilhac	Norman Marshall	Globe
May	The Tempest	William Shakespeare	Ferdinand	George Devine and Marius Goring	Old Vic
Sep/Dec	Thunder Rock	Robert Ardrey	Charleston	Herbert Marshall	Tour
1942					
Dec	Flare Path	Terence Rattigan	Flight-Lieutenant Graham	Margaret Webster	Henry Miller, New York
1945					
Apr	Hearts of Oak	a pageant	Nelson		Albert Hall
1946					
Jun	The Brothers Karamazov	Theodore Dostoevsky adapted by Alec Guinness	Mitya Karamazov	Peter Brook	Lyric, Hammersmith
Jul	Vicious Circle	Jean-Paul Sartre translated by Marjorie Gabain and Joan Swinstead	Garcin	Peter Brook	Arts

† The Witch of Edmonton *was written by Thomas Dekker, William Rowley and*
John Ford. The Old Vic programme named Thomas Dekker as sole author.

DATE	TITLE	PLAYWRIGHT	ROLE	DIRECTOR	THEATRE
1946/1948 The Old Vic Company at the New Theatre					
Sep	King Lear	William Shakespeare	Fool	Laurence Olivier	
Oct	An Inspector Calls	J.B. Priestley	Eric Birling	Basil Dean	
Nov	Cyrano de Bergerac	Edmond Rostand translated by Brian Hooker	Comte de Guiche	Tyrone Guthrie	
1947					
Jan	The Alchemist	Ben Jonson	Abel Drugger	John Burrell	
Apr	Richard II	William Shakespeare	Richard II	Ralph Richardson	
Dec	Saint Joan	George Bernard Shaw	The Dauphin	John Burrell	
1948					
Feb	The Government Inspector	Nikolai V. Gogol translated and adapted by D.J. Campbell	Hlestakov	John Burrell	
Mar	Coriolanus	William Shakespeare	Menenius Agrippa	E.Martin Browne	
Sep	Twelfth Night	William Shakespeare		Alec Guinness†	
1949					
Feb	The Human Touch	J.Lee Thompson and Dudley Leslie	Dr James Simpson	Peter Ashmore	Savoy
Aug	The Cocktail Party	T.S. Eliot	Sir Henry Harcourt-Reilly	E. Martin Browne	Lyceum, Edinburgh
1950					
Jan	The Cocktail Party	T.S. Eliot	Sir Henry Harcourt-Reilly	E. Martin Browne	Henry Miller, New York
1951					
May	Hamlet	William Shakespeare	Hamlet	Alec Guinness and Frank Hauser	New
1952					
Apr	Under the Sycamore Tree	Sam and Bella Spewack	The Ant Scientist	Peter Glenville	Aldwych
1953 Shakespeare Playhouse, Stratford, Ontario, Canada					
Jul	All's Well That Ends Well	William Shakespeare	King of France	Tyrone Guthrie	
Jul	Richard III	William Shakespeare	Richard III	Tyrone Guthrie	
1954					
Mar	The Prisoner	Bridget Boland	The Cardinal	Peter Glenville	Globe
1956					
May	Hotel Paradiso	Georges Feydeau and Maurice Desvallières translated by Peter Glenville	Boniface	Peter Glenville	Winter Garden
1960					
May	Ross	Terence Rattigan	T.E. Lawrence	Glen Byam Shaw	Theatre Royal, Haymarket
1963					
Sep	Exit the King	Eugene Ionesco translated by Donald Watson	Beringer	George Devine	Lyceum, Edinburgh
	Exit the King	Eugene Ionesco translated by Donald Watson	Beringer	George Devine	Royal Court
1964					
Jan	Dylan	Sidney Michaels	Dylan Thomas	Peter Glenville	Plymouth, New York
1966					
Jan	Incident at Vichy	Arthur Miller	Von Berg	Peter Wood	Phoenix
Oct	Macbeth	William Shakespeare	Macbeth	William Gaskill	Royal Court
1967					
Oct	Wise Child	Simon Gray	'Mrs Artminster'		Wyndham's
1968					
Jun	The Cocktail Party	T.S. Eliot	Sir Henry Harcourt-Reilly	Alec Guinness	Chichester
Nov	The Cocktail Party	T.S. Eliot	Sir Henry Harcourt-Reilly	Alec Guinness	Wyndham's
1969					
Feb	The Cocktail Party	T.S. Eliot	Sir Henry Harcourt-Reilly	Alec Guinness	Theatre Royal, Haymarket
1970					
Jul	Time Out of Mind	Bridget Boland	John	Stephen Barry	Yvonne Arnaud, Guildford
1971					
Aug	A Voyage Round My Father	John Mortimer	Father	Ronald Eyre	Theatre Royal, Haymarket
1973					
May	Habeas Corpus	Alan Bennett	Dr Arthur Wicksteed	Ronald Eyre	Lyric
1975					
Apr	A Family and A Fortune	Julian Mitchell adapted from novel by Ivy Compton-Burnett	Dudley Gaveston	Alan Strachan	Apollo
1976					
Oct	Yahoo	Jonathan Swift adapted by Alec Guinness and Alan Strachan	Dr Jonathan Swift	Alan Strachan	Queen's
1977					
Sep	The Old Country	Alan Bennett	Hilary	Clifford Williams	Queen's
1984	The Merchant of Venice	William Shakespeare	Shylock	Patrick Garland	Chichester
1988					
Nov	A Walk in the Woods	Lee Blessing	Andrey Lvovich Botvinnik	Ronald Eyre	Comedy

† Twelfth Night. *Alec Guinness only directed the play; he did not appear in it.*

FILM

DATE	FILM	ROLE	SCREENPLAY	DIRECTOR
1934	Evensong	Extra	Edward Knoblock and Dorothy Farnum based on play by Edward Knoblock and Beverley Nichols	Victor Saville
1946	Great Expectations	Herbert Pocket	David Lean and Ronald Neame based on novel by Charles Dickens	David Lean
1948	Oliver Twist	Fagin	David Lean and Stanley Haynes based on novel by Charles Dickens	David Lean
1949	Kind Hearts and Coronets	The Duke The Banker The Parson The General The Admiral Young d'Ascoyne Young Henry Lady Agatha	Robert Hamer and John Dighton from novel *Israel Rank* by Roy Horniman	Robert Hamer
	A Run For Your Money	Whimple	Richard Hughes, Charles Frend and Leslie Norman based on original story by Clifford Evans	Charles Frend
1950	The Last Holiday	George Bird	J.B. Priestley	Henry Cass
	The Mudlark	Disraeli	Nunnally Johnson based on novel by Theodore Bonnet	Jean Negulesco
1951	The Lavender Hill Mob	Holland	T.E.B. Clarke	Charles Crichton
	The Man in the White Suit	Sidney Stratton	Roger Macdougall, John Dighton and Alexander Mackendrick from play by Roger Macdougall	Alexander Mackendrick
1952	The Card (US title: The Promotor)	Edward Henry ('Denry') Machin	Eric Ambler from novel by Arnold Bennett	Ronald Neame
1953	Malta Story	Flight-Lieutenant Peter Ross	William Fairchild and Nigel Balchin	Brian Desmond Hurst
	The Square Mile	Narrator	J.M. Matthews	Diana Pine
	The Captain's Paradise	Captain Henry St James	Alec Coppel and Nicholas Phipps	Anthony Kimmins
1954	Father Brown (US title: The Detective)	Father Brown	Thelma Schnee and Robert Hamer based on stories by G.K. Chesterton	Robert Hamer
	Stratford Adventure	Himself	Gudrun Parker	Morten Parker
1955	To Paris With Love	Colonel Sir Edgar Fraser	Robert Buckner	Robert Hamer
	The Prisoner	The Cardinal	Bridget Boland from her play	Peter Glenville
	The Ladykillers	The Professor	William Rose	Alexander Mackendrick
1956	Richardson's England	Narrator	John Hawkesworth and Robert Hamer	John Hawkesworth
	The Swan	Prince Albert	John Dighton from play by Ferenc Molnar	Charles Vidor
1957	The Bridge on the River Kwai	Colonel Nicholson	Pierre Boulle from his novel	David Lean
	Barnacle Bill (US title: All at Sea)	William Horatio Ambrose and six ancestors	T.E.B. Clarke	Charles Frend
1958	The Horse's Mouth	Gulley Jimson	Alec Guinness from novel by Joyce Cary	Ronald Neame
	The Scapegoat	John Barratt Count Jacques de Gue	Robert Hamer adapted by Gore Vidal from novel by Daphne du Maurier	Robert Hamer
1959	Our Man in Havana	Jim Wormold	Graham Greene from his novel	Carol Reed
1960	Tunes of Glory	Lieutenant-Colonel Jock Sinclair	James Kennaway from his novel	Ronald Neame
1961	A Majority of One	Koichi Asano	Leonard Spigelgass from his play	Mervyn LeRoy
1962	H.M.S. Defiant (US title: Damn the Defiant)	Captain Crawford	Nigel Kneale and Edmund H. North from novel *Mutiny* by Frank Tilsley	Lewis Gilbert
	Lawrence of Arabia	Prince Feisal	Robert Bolt	David Lean
1964	The Fall of the Roman Empire	Marcus Aurelius	Ben Barzman, Basilio Franchina and Philip Jordan	Anthony Mann
1965	Situation Hopeless – But Not Serious	Herr Frick	Silvia Reinhardt from novel *The Hiding Place* by Robert Shaw	Gottfried Reinhardt
	Doctor Zhivago	Yevgraf Zhivago	Robert Bolt from novel by Boris Leonidovic Pasternak	David Lean
1966	Hotel Paradiso	Benedict Boniface	Peter Glenville and Jean-Claude Carrière adapted from play *L'Hotel du Libre Echange* by Georges Feydeau and Maurice Desvallières	Peter Glenville
	The Quiller Memorandum	Pol	Harold Pinter from novel *The Berlin Memorandum* by Adam Hall	Michael Anderson
1968	The Comedians	Major Jones	Graham Greene from his novel	Peter Glenville
1970	Cromwell	King Charles I	Ken Hughes	Ken Hughes
	Scrooge	Marley's Ghost	Leslie Bricusse musical based on *A Christmas Carol* by Charles Dickens	Ronald Neame
1972	Fratello Sole, Sorella Luna (English title: Brother Sun, Sister Moon)	Pope Innocent III	Suso Cecchi D'Amico, Kenneth Ross, Lina Wertmuller and Franco Zeffirelli	Franco Zeffirelli
1973	Hitler – The Last Ten Days	Adolf Hitler	Ennio de Concinci, Maria Pia Fusco, Wolfgang Reinhardt based on eye-witness account *The Last Days of the Chancellery* by Gerhard Boldt. English Screenplay adaptation: Ivan Moffat	Ennio de Concinci
	Murder by Death	Bensonmum	Neil Simon	Robert Moore
1977	Star Wars	Ben (Obi-Wan) Kenobi	George Lucas	George Lucas
1980	The Empire Strikes Back	Ben (Obi-Wan) Kenobi	Leigh Brackett and Lawrence Kasdan from story by George Lucas	Irvin Kershner

DATE	FILM	ROLE	SCREENPLAY	DIRECTOR
	Raise the Titanic	John Bigalow	Adam Kennedy from novel by Clive Cussler	Jerry Jameson
	Little Lord Fauntleroy*	Earl of Dorincourt	Blanche Hanalis from novel by Frances Eliza Hodgson Burnett	Jack Gold
1983	Lovesick	Sigmund Freud	Marshall Brickman	Marshall Brickman
	Return of the Jedi	Ben (Obi-Wan) Kenobi	Lawrence Kasdan and George Lucas from story by George Lucas	Richard Marquand
1984	A Passage to India	Professor Godbole	David Lean from novel by E.M. Forster and play by Santha Rami Rau	David Lean
1987	Little Dorrit	William Dorrit	Christine Edzard from novel by Charles Dickens	Christine Edzard
1988	A Handful of Dust	Mr Todd	Tim Sullivan, Derek Granger and Charles Sturridge from novel by Evelyn Waugh	Charles Sturridge

* Little Lord Fauntleroy *was made for American television but shown in cinemas abroad.*

TELEVISION

DATE	TITLE	ROLE	WRITER	DIRECTOR	COMPANY
1955	Baker's Dozen	The Major	'Saki' (H.H. Munro)	Desmond Davis	ITV
1959	The Wicked Scheme of Jebal Deeks	Jebal Deeks	John D. Hess	Franklin Shaffer	CBS
1969	Conversation at Night	The Executioner	Friedrich Durrenmatt translated by Robert David MacDonald	Rudolph Cartier	BBC
1970	Twelfth Night	Malvolio	William Shakespeare	John Dexter	ATV
1972	Solo	recital	e.e. cummings	James Cellan Jones	BBC
	Solo	recital	T.S. Eliot	James Cellan Jones	BBC
1974	The Gift of Friendship	Jocelyn Broome	John Osborne	Mike Newell	Yorkshire
1977	Caesar and Cleopatra	Julius Caesar	George Bernard Shaw	James Cellan Jones	Southern
1979	Tinker, Tailor, Soldier, Spy	George Smiley	Arthur Hopcraft from novel by John Le Carré	John Irvin	BBC
1980	Little Lord Fauntleroy*	Earl of Dorincourt	Blanche Hanalis from novel by Frances Eliza Hodgson Burnett	Jack Gold	US
	The Morecambe and Wise Christmas Show	Guest Artist	Eddie Braben	John Ammonds	Thames
1982	Smiley's People	George Smiley	John Hopkins and John Le Carré from novel by John Le Carré	Simon Langton	BBC
1984	Edwin	Sir Fennimore Truscott	John Mortimer	Rodney Bennett	Anglia
1985	Monsignor Quixote	Father Quixote	Christopher Neame from novel by Graham Greene	Rodney Bennett	Thames

* Little Lord Fauntleroy *was made for American television but shown in cinemas abroad.*

RECORDINGS

TITLE	COMPANY	TITLE	COMPANY
major recordings include:		A Leaden Anthology	Jupiter
The Argo Treasury of English Poetry from Hardy to Eliot	Argo	More Favourite Poems	Argo
British Poetry of Our Time: T.S. Eliot	Argo	The Poems of T.S. Eliot	PLP
Christian Poetry and Prose	Jupiter	Sir Alec Guinness: A Personal Choice	RCA-Victor
The Cocktail Party by T.S. Eliot	Bruswick	The Waste Land and other Poems by T.S. Eliot	Argo
		Your Favourite Poems	Argo

RADIO

All productions for the BBC

1938   Doctor Faustus
        The Snowman

1939   The Seagull
        Scenes from Romeo and Juliet

1940   The Tempest
        This is Illyria, Lady

1941   A Month in the Country

1942   Distant Point
        The Rape of the Lock
        Twelfth Night
        The Fort

1946   He Was Born Gay
        A Time for Verse
        Fourth Form Feature
        Doctor Faustus
        Vicious Circle
        Theatre Programme No 2
        The Story of the Nativity

1947   A Time for Verse
        King Richard II
        Britain's Pleasure Parade

1949   Antigone
        Interview on Kind Hearts and Coronets

1950   A Christmas Carol

1951   Interview on The Man in the White Suit

1952   Woman's Hour
        Henry Hall's Guest Night

1955   What Goes On

1960   In Town Tonight
        Desert Island Discs
        The John Mills Story

1963   The Hunting of the Snark

1965   Poems by T.S. Eliot

1967   Ten to Eight

1968   The World This Weekend

1971   A Voyage Round My Father (extract)

1974   My Own Right Hand Shall Do It
        King Lear

1975   A Family and A Fortune (extract)
        The Waste Land
        Journey of the Magi

1976   Interview by Derek Parker

1977   Desert Island Discs

1979   Confessions of a Primary Terrestrial Mental
        Receiver and Communicator

1984   The Merchant of Venice (extract)

1985   Interview by John Dunn
        Woman's Hour

ACKNOWLEDGEMENTS

The author would like to begin by thanking the photographers, his editor Ian Hyde, his designer Hugh Schermuly, and Susanne McDadd and Tim Pearce of Harrap.

The author and publisher would like to express their appreciation to the following for their assistance and/or permission to reproduce the photographs. Every effort has been made to trace the copyright owners and the author and publisher would like to apologise to anyone whose copyright has been infringed.

ABPC/Watergate, 66; Anglia Television Limited, 152; ATV, 128; Sophie Baker, 129; copyright BBC Enterprises, 146; British Lion, 79; Samuel Bronston, 112; Columbia Pictures Corporation, 2, 13, 82, 85, 92, 94, 130, 140; Columbia/Horizon, 110; Columbia/GW, 109; Columbia/Kingsmead, 102; Howard Coster, 16, 19; Curzon, 147, 156; Ealing Films, 6, 11, 56, 58, 59, 62, 63, 70, 71, 72, 73, 86, 88, 96; EMI, 154; GFD/British Film Makers, 78; GFD/Two Cities, 84; Lord Grade, 150 (top); John Haynes, 103, 118, 127, 132, 133, 136, 137, 138, 141, 142, 158; Hulton Picture Library, 14, 30, 32, 37, 45; Sandra Lousada, 111; The Raymond Mander and Joe Mitchenson Theatre Collection, 22, 25 (right), 29, 33; Angus McBean, courtesy of Harvard Theater Collection, 9, 36, 39, 74, 80, 81, 104, 116, 124; MGM-EMI, 90, 100, 115, 120, 126, 135; The National Film Archive, 2, 6, 11, 12, 13, 35, 44, 53, 54, 56, 58, 59, 62, 63, 67, 70, 71, 72, 73, 75, 78, 79, 82, 84, 85, 86, 88, 90, 92, 94, 96, 98, 99, 100, 102, 106, 107, 108, 109, 110, 112, 114, 115, 120, 121, 126, 130, 131, 134, 135, 140, 147, 148, 150, 154, 156, 160; National Portrait Gallery, London (Howard Coster Collection), 19; Paramount Pictures Ltd, 114, 134; Popperfoto, 31, 122, 123; Premier, 157; The Rank Organisation plc, 35, 44, 53, 54, 75, 121; Rex Features Ltd, 113, 145; Houston Rogers by courtesy of the Trustees of The Theatre Museum, Victoria and Albert Museum, 16, 20, 25 (left), 26, 27, 28, 68; Norman Rosemont, 148; RPTA (Richard Price Television Associates Limited), 144; Sasha, 16; Shakespeare Centre Library, Stratford-upon-Avon, 17, 21; Southern Television Ltd, 144; Thames Television, 155; John Timbers, 10; Times Newspapers Ltd, 15, 16, 34, 38, 60, 76, 77, 151; Twentieth Century-Fox, 67; United Artists, 98, 99; UA/Knightsbridge, 12, 106, 107; John Vickers Archive, 8, 40, 41, 42, 43, 46, 48, 49, 50, 51, 52; Warner Bros, 108, 150 (bottom); Weintraub, 6, 11, 56, 58, 59, 62, 63, 70, 71, 72, 73, 79, 86, 88, 96; Peter Waugh, 91; West Sussex Gazette, 153.

The author would like to add a personal note of thanks to Anita Appel, Brian Baxter, Laurence Bernes, Suzanne Common, Sheila Formoy and H. M. Tennent Ltd, John Haynes, Peter Hirst, Glenn Night, Colin Lesley, Angus McKay, Amanda Malpass, Joe Mitchenson, Alison Rogers, Jonathan Vickers, Mary White, Jane Wilkinson, and everybody at the BFI stills and reference library.

INDEX